A Change is Going to Come

Growing up in the 60s

Charles Vaughn

ISBN: Hardcover - 9781969066115
Paperback - 9781969066108
Ebook - 9781969066092

Published by

Columbus Book Publishers
www.columbusbookpublishers.com

Printed in the United States of America

Dedication

This book is dedicated to all those who grew up during the turbulent times of the 1960s—a generation that witnessed both profound struggle and remarkable transformation. To my family, from whom I draw my inspiration and strength, who taught me to see the world with both clear eyes and an open heart.

To those service men and women who never received a homecoming, whose stories remain untold but not forgotten. Their courage in the face of adversity continues to light the way forward.

Understand that the life I lead is inspired by their sacrifices, taking nothing for granted and honoring the days they did not get. In every word of this book, I carry their legacy—a testament to resilience, truth, and the enduring power of memory.

For those who were there, and for those who will never forget.

Acknowledgment

To my fellow members of the Class of 1969, who shared those formative years that shaped who we would become. We came of age during a time of profound change—when the world seemed to shift beneath our feet almost daily, yet somehow we found our footing together.

To those who sat beside me in classrooms where we wrestled with ideas that would define our generation, who walked the same hallways during those pivotal years when everything felt both possible and uncertain. You were there during the late-night conversations that stretched until dawn, the moments of doubt when the future seemed unclear, and the celebrations when dreams felt within reach.

We graduated into a world that demanded we grow up quickly, and many of us scattered to pursue different paths— some to college, others to work, still others to serve our country. Though life took us in different directions, the bonds forged during those crucial years remained. The values we debated, the hopes we shared, and the challenges we faced together became the foundation upon which we built our adult lives.

To those classmates who remained lifelong friends and

to those whose paths diverged from mine but who remain part of my story—thank you. The person I became was shaped not just by my own experiences, but by witnessing your courage, your struggles, your successes, and your resilience.

Class of 1969, we were more than just people who happened to graduate together. We were witnesses to each other's becoming, and for that gift of shared growth and mutual influence, I remain forever grateful.

About the Author

Charles Vaughn was born in Ottumwa, Iowa in 1950, the youngest of three sons. After graduating from Ottumwa High School in 1969, he enlisted in the United States Navy, where he served aboard the USS Midway. Upon completion of his service, he worked at the local hospital, splitting time between the emergency room, coronary care unit, and surgical wing, eventually following a family physician to Arizona working as a Physician Assistant.

Charles met and married his wife Denice in 1974. He obtained an Associate of Arts degree in Liberal Studies and later accepted a full-time position with the National Guard in 1979, retiring in 1996. He and his wife of 50 years have raised two daughters, Meredith and Maggie, and now enjoy the company of three grandchildren.

The Vaughns have been residents of Arizona since 1998, settling in Gilbert in 2001. After a lifetime of experiences, Charles Vaughn turned to writing, publishing his debut novel, "In Our Righteous Might," in 2023. This work marks the beginning of his literary career, drawing upon his rich background in military service and family life.

With his unique perspective shaped by military service,

healthcare experience, family values, and Midwestern roots, Charles Vaughn brings authenticity and depth to his storytelling, creating narratives that resonate with readers across generations.

Table of Contents

Preface

The past can never be silenced as it echoes through our present in ways both subtle and profound, shaping who we are even as we imagine ourselves freed from its influence. Some chapters of our collective story speak more loudly than others—their lessons refusing to fade, their questions remaining unanswered. The eight years spanning from that November day in Dallas to the tumultuous in the fall of 1971 constitute such a chapter.

This book is historically correct as it closely follows the accounts of the times. It offers no scholarly pretense of objectivity, no distanced analysis of policy decisions or military strategies. Instead, these pages contain something more intimate and perhaps more revealing: a family's journey from the youngest son, Phillips prospective, through the crucible that forged modern America. Their story mirrors the nation's own transformation during those years.

In a modest Iowa town, far from the corridors of power and the urban epicenters of protest, the McManus family experienced America's coming of age through their own. Parents who had weathered Depression and war watched as their children encountered questions, they themselves had never been permitted to ask. Those children—born into unprecedented prosperity and promise—awakened to realities that challenged everything they had been taught to believe about their country and themselves.

Between Camelot's end and the shadow of Vietnam lies this chronicle of youth finding its voice. While rockets reached for the moon, voices rose in the streets. While bombs fell overseas, new freedoms were claimed at home.

The soundtrack of revolution played on transistor radios as dinner table conversations became ideological battlegrounds where love was tested but never broken.

This is a combination of factual as well as fictional stories, shaped by memories of the story teller. Names have been changed, certain events compressed or expanded in service of the larger truth this story seeks to tell. But the essential journey—that of idealism tested by reality, innocence seasoned by experience, and the discovery that freedom demands both courage and responsibility—remains faithful to the lived experiences of countless American families during this pivotal era.

The generation that came of age in these years has been alternately glorified and diminished, their struggles romanticized and dismissed.

Unlike their parents, the greatest generation" for their sacrifice and unity of purpose, the baby boomers inherited a nation of contradictions.

They did not face a single, identifiable enemy but rather confronted the gap between

America's ideals and its practices. They questioned authority not out of rebellion alone, but because circumstances demanded new answers to enduring questions about justice, equality, and the true meaning of liberty.

I offer this story now, decades later, when the passions of that era have cooled but its unresolved tensions remain. As new generations face their own crucible moments, perhaps there is wisdom to be found in how one family navigated their own—how they broke and mended, doubted and believed, struggled and ultimately persevered through years that changed everything.

For those who lived through these times, may these pages honor your journey without simplifying its complexity. For those born after, may this help you understand not just what happened, but how it felt to be alive when America confronted itself and emerged, wounded but wiser, into a new chapter of its unfinished story.

The struggles recounted here must not be forgotten, nor should the awakening they represent be diminished. In the McManus family's story lives the most American of narratives: the never-ending work of becoming who we aspire to be, both as individuals and as a nation.

Chapter 1: Loss of Innocence

It was the kind of day that felt timeless in a small Iowa town—calm, comfortable. A typical autumn day in November. Anna had the house to herself for a few precious hours, and she moved through her tasks with practiced ease. The steady rhythm of the iron gliding across Jim's shirts mingled with the soft ticking of the kitchen clock. Outside, snow fell gently, blurring the outlines of the bare trees and coating the yard in a fresh white layer.

She paused for a moment, wiped her brow with the corner of her apron, and looked out the window. The neighborhood was quiet—just the way she liked it. The roast was already in the oven, filling the air with a savory warmth, and a pot of navy beans was soaking near the stove for tomorrow's dinner.

Her thoughts wandered to the boys. Raymond, her oldest son, had a big history test today, she remembered. Art, named after her brother, had been nervously talking about a presentation in English. Phillip, the youngest, had insisted he didn't need help with his math homework last night—but she wasn't so sure.

1

Anna had just finished preparing her lunch and sat down to watch the midday news when a special bulletin interrupted the broadcast: President Kennedy had been shot.

The anchor's voice was shaky, clearly struggling to remain composed as details were still coming in.
Anna froze, her fork halfway to her mouth, the sound of the television loud in the sudden silence of the kitchen.

Her heart skipped—the President? Shot? She set the fork down gently on the edge of her plate, not taking her eyes off the screen.

The anchor continued, "We do not have confirmed information on the President's condition at this time. Repeat, President Kennedy has been shot in Dallas, Texas. He was riding in an open limousine along with the First Lady, Jacqueline Kennedy, and Texas Governor John Connally."

Anna's hand trembled as she reached for the volume knob, turning it up. The screen cut to footage of crowds scattering, police running, people screaming. Her mind raced. Jim. The boys. They'd be hearing about this soon, too.

She stood and instinctively reached for the phone on the wall, unsure of who she meant to call. Jim at the post office?

The school?

Maybe her mother, Mary, to see if she had heard. She just needed to hear another voice—someone to confirm it, to help process what was happening.

Outside, the snow kept falling—quiet and unaware. But inside, the world had just changed.

Anna was still watching the news unfold when Walter Cronkite, visibly shaken and with tears in his eyes, announced that President Kennedy had died at 1:00 p.m. CST from a gunshot wound to the head.

Anna's gaze locked onto the flickering screen, her trembling hands clutching the chair as tears streaked down her face.

Her breath hitched, and she dropped the plate she was holding, shards scattering across the floor.

"No," she whispered, almost to herself, her voice cracking under the weight of disbelief.

The young President who had offered such hope for America's future was dead.

The same announcement came over the school's PA system. After a moment of silence and the Pledge of Allegiance, school was dismissed early and announced it would remain closed through the Thanksgiving holidays.

Art and Phillip slowly walked home, neither saying much, both trying to comprehend who could have done such a thing, how it could have happened, and how devastated their mother would be.

They walked side by side, the weight of the announcement still hanging in the air. Their thoughts were tangled, trying to make sense of the tragedy just revealed over the loudspeaker. The silence between them wasn't uncomfortable—it was a shared space of disbelief.

Neither had spoken much during the walk, too wrapped up in their own thoughts. What had happened? Who would do something like that? The questions pressed down on them like an invisible weight.

Art kicked at a loose rock on the sidewalk, his gaze fixed ahead but not really seeing anything.

Phillip, on the other hand, kept looking up at the sky, as if hoping the answers might fall from the clouds. Neither of them could understand how something so unimaginable could affect their family—let alone their mother, who had always been so strong.

"She... she's going to be devastated," Art finally said, his voice low and shaky.

Phillip nodded but didn't respond. He couldn't bring himself to say the words they were both thinking—the fear of how their mother would react was too real, too sharp.

The closer they got to home, the more they felt the weight of the unknown pressing down on them, each step feeling like a march toward something they couldn't fully prepare for. The holidays had never seemed further away.

They walked into the house quietly, almost cautiously, unsure of what they'd find.

The television's glow flickered across the dim living room, and there she was—Mom—curled on the edge of the couch, tears streaming down her face, her body trembling with sobs she couldn't seem to control. The sound of the news droned on in the background, but it was her grief that filled the room.

Art and Phillip froze in the doorway, unsure how to move, what to say, or even if they should say anything at all. Then, without a word, they stepped forward and sat beside her, one on each side.

Art gently took her left hand, and Phillip wrapped his fingers around her right. They didn't speak. They didn't need to.

The TV showed the same footage on repeat—police cars, flashing lights, a scrolling banner with breaking news updates. It was surreal, like something out of a movie.

But it wasn't. It was real.
And it was happening to them.

Time moved slowly. Minutes felt like hours. The house was unnaturally quiet except for the hum of the news and the occasional sniffle from their mother. It would be a while before Jim made it home from work, and Raymond—still at the high school—was stuck waiting for the bus, probably hearing the same updates from a different TV in a crowded room.

The three of them sat there, clinging to each other in the middle of a world that suddenly didn't make sense. There were no words, only the quiet comfort of being together when everything else felt like it was falling apart.

On Sunday, Anna insisted they all go to church. The pastor of the Plymouth Congregational Church—the same one the family had attended since Jim and Anna were married—tried to make sense of what they had seen. He reminded them that it was okay not to understand.

The pastor said, "It is times like this we must turn to God

with our questions. Why did He let this happen? How does this fit in Your plan? I stand here today and confess that I do not know." His voice rose as he declared, "It is okay not to understand."

But Phillip couldn't focus on what the pastor was saying. His mind couldn't shake the image of the funeral procession. As he closed his eyes, the sound of hooves against pavement echoed in his thoughts. *How could God allow this to happen?* he wondered.

On the way home, Jim tried to help him understand.

"God is good, but He allows evil because of free will," Jim said. "I don't have all the answers, son. But I believe that with free will comes the power to choose—and sometimes, people make the wrong choices."

Jim didn't know if any of it made sense to his youngest son, but he understood—after his own time in the war—that everyone handles grief in their own way. And Phillip needed the space to work through it in his.

They walked in from church, hung up their coats, and turned on the TV. As they sat down, the news was covering the transfer of Lee Harvey Oswald—the main suspect in President Kennedy's assassination—from the city jail to the

Dallas County jail. Suddenly, a nightclub owner named Jack Ruby stepped through the crowd and, at point-blank range, shot and killed Oswald live on national television.

"Oh my God," Anna whispered. "They're killing him. Why?"

As they watched Ruby shoot Oswald, Phillip felt something inside him shift permanently. The world he'd believed in—where good people were safe and bad people got caught—suddenly seemed like a child's fantasy. In its place stood something darker, more complicated, more frightening. He glanced at his mother's face and saw the same realization reflected there.

This shocking event only deepened the public's suspicion and fueled conspiracy theories. Why did Ruby do it? What was his connection to Oswald? Was it an impulsive act, or was he part of a larger plot?

For many, the live footage of Oswald's shooting—along with relentless news coverage and countless newspaper articles—planted a growing belief that Oswald had not acted alone. It was a belief Phillip would come to share.

These became three sleepless nights, forever etched into the memories of anyone who lived through that time.

As the family gathered around the television, no one moved to turn on the lamps despite the growing darkness. The blue glow of the screen illuminated their faces—Jim's jaw clenched tight, Anna's eyes red-rimmed, the boys unnaturally still.

When the image of John-John's salute appeared, Anna let out a sound somewhere between a gasp and a sob. Jim's hand found hers in the darkness.

The hours turned into days, and the family rarely left the living room, bearing witness to history unfolding on their television screen. Like millions around the world, they watched in stunned silence as the tragic events played out. The swearing-in of Vice President Johnson. The flag-draped coffin being unloaded at Andrews Air Force Base, with Jackie standing by in her blood-stained dress as her husband's body was placed in the hearse. Jackie kneeling beside the casket, kissing the flag covering it.

The funeral procession moved with devastating precision down Pennsylvania Avenue—the rhythmic cadence of muffled drums echoing through their living room. The riderless horse, boots reversed in the stirrups, pranced nervously behind the caisson. Representatives from each military branch marched in perfect, practiced unison.

Crowds stood shoulder to shoulder along the route, handkerchiefs pressed to faces, hats held over hearts—their collective grief spilling into the streets of Washington.

They watched as the Kennedy family walked quietly behind the caisson.

The sight of Jackie—all in black, her face obscured by a dark veil—clutching Robert Kennedy's hand, sent a fresh wave of grief through the room.

Behind her somber figure walked the brothers, sisters, and close friends of the fallen president, their footsteps measured and heavy as they made their final journey to Arlington. The simple human gesture of Jackie holding her brother-in-law's hand for support seemed to embody the nation's collective need to find something solid to grasp onto in the midst of such destabilizing loss. Anna found herself leaning slightly toward Jim on the couch, their shoulders touching—seeking that same quiet reassurance. The muffled notes of *Taps* drifted through the cold November air, hauntingly beautiful in their simplicity, annotating the final goodbye from a grateful nation.

When the 21-gun salute began—sharp cracks followed

by the deeper boom of cannon volleys—everyone in the living room flinched, the sudden violence of the sound a stark reminder of the violence that had brought them to this moment. Phillip noticed his mother's hand tighten around his father's, her knuckles white. Even through the television's small speaker, those shots seemed to echo across the country, reaching into their quiet Iowa home and shattering what little composure they had managed to hold.

After the president was laid to rest, Anna turned her attention to the approaching holidays, determined to make them feel as normal as possible despite the lingering heaviness in the air. The days blurred together in the wake of tragedy, but as the sun set on Sunday, Anna felt a quiet resolve. It was time to face the world again.

She focused on the family meal, on all the little traditions leading up to it. That evening, they would bundle up and go choose their Christmas tree—something they'd done every Thanksgiving night since the boys were small.

The family all knew she was keeping busy to give her mind something else to focus on—anything to distract from the tremendous loss she had endured. Like Phillip, she had to find her own way of moving through the grief.

Phillip had become an avid reader of the local *Ottumwa*

Courier, much to the irritation of his father, who often came home from work only to find the paper misplaced—again—before supper.

Thanksgiving arrived, and though the menu was traditional, the excitement just wasn't there. No matter how hard everyone tried, something about the day felt off. They recognized the

rituals of their past but felt the absence of the joy and security that had once accompanied them. And the world was changing—and the quiet innocence of the place they'd always felt comfortable in was changing with it. Phillip had also discovered, earlier, that there was no Santa Claus or Easter Bunny. And now, he knew something far more sobering: not all stories have happy endings.

Chapter 2: From Camelot to Chaos

The world seemed to be changing at breakneck speed as America struggled to move on from the assassination of President Kennedy. What began as a crisp, hopeful autumn day in Dallas—November 22, 1963—ended in national shock and mourning. Television brought the tragedy into every American living room in an unprecedented way. Walter Cronkite, removing his thick black glasses, his voice cracking as he announced the president's death, became an indelible image etched into the country's collective memory.

As weeks turned into months, questions piled up—many unanswered—and a sense of distrust began to spread. Around dinner tables and in barbershops, whispered theories and heated debates revealed a growing suspicion of the official accounts. The assassination profoundly affected American youth, many of whom had seen their parents weep openly in front of the television, transfixed by the somber funeral procession and the haunting image of young John-John's salute.

Kennedy's call to service had inspired a generation—and his sudden loss left them disillusioned, uncertain whether the political establishment could ever be trusted again.

Phillip had always been more interested in politics than his brothers. He remembered clearly the campaign work he and Art had done for Kennedy and Johnson back in 1960. Though only ten years old, the memory remained vivid—the feel of the crisp campaign flyers in his hands, the nervous excitement of knocking on strangers' doors. Jim would drop them off at one end of a block while the boys canvassed the neighborhood, distributing literature about the young senator from Massachusetts and his running mate.

The leaflets—patriotically colored in red, white, and blue—were neatly packed into *Des Moines Register* paper bags, the same ones they used for their morning routes. Jim, pipe in hand, would watch patiently from the car before driving them to the next street. The leaves crunched beneath their feet as they moved from porch to porch, a pair of boys feeling important, like they were helping shape the future.

Phillip often clashed with his fourth-grade nemesis, Tim, a devout Nixon supporter. One day, while their teacher, Mrs. Hannah, played piano in class and asked for song requests,

Tim suggested *The Battle Hymn of the Republic.* Phillip immediately countered, requesting *The Battle Hymn of the Democrats.* A few days later, to their parents' surprise and amusement, Mrs. Hannah had the anecdote published in the *Courier*'s editorial page.

Phillip and Art could still recall their excitement on election night, when their mother woke them to announce Kennedy's victory. Raymond, older and less enthralled by politics, chose sleep over history.

The two younger boys huddled around the black-and-white television in their pajamas, eyes wide with wonder as they watched the broadcast. Their mother stood behind them, a gentle hand resting on Phillip's shoulder. Through the static, the crowd's cheers filtered in, and Kennedy's Boston accent rang out during his victory speech.

"Do you think things will be different now?" Phillip whispered to Art, not fully understanding, but sensing the moment's weight.

"Mom says he's the youngest president ever elected. And the first Catholic too."

Anna smiled. "Remember this night, boys. Someday, you'll tell your children you watched Kennedy win."

On Inauguration Day, their mother let them stay home from school to witness history unfold. She believed it was an experience worth seeing with their own eyes. As Kennedy delivered his inaugural address, Phillip listened with unusual intensity. When the president said, *"Ask not what your country can do for you, ask what you can do for your country,"* Phillip turned to Anna and said, "Someday, those words will be in history books."

In that moment, a seed was planted that would one day send him off to serve.

When the Warren Commission finally released its report in September 1964—nearly ten months after that dark day in Dallas—its conclusion that Lee Harvey Oswald had acted alone failed to satisfy many. Phillip was among them.

Sitting at the kitchen table with the Sunday paper spread out before him, he voiced his doubts to his father.

"I don't believe our president was killed by just one man," he said quietly but firmly.

Jim, weary from a long week at the post office, lowered his coffee cup. "What makes you think that?" His tone wasn't dismissive—just tired. He was of a generation that had seen the horrors of war and now watched the world grow increasingly unstable.

"If you watch the footage, someone shot from the front. Why would Mrs. Kennedy climb to the back of the car if the shots came from behind? It doesn't make sense, Dad."

"You're too young to understand," Jim replied, folding the paper slowly. "Sometimes there are no good answers."

But Phillip held his father's gaze, his eyes no longer those of a child. "I know what I saw. And nothing will change that."

In that moment, something shifted. Phillip had not only lost his childhood innocence, but discovered the unsettling power of doubt. The comforting certainties of youth were slipping away, replaced by a more complicated view of government and truth.
The kitchen clock ticked steadily behind them, marking time in a world forever changed.

The Warren Report raised more questions than it answered. Phillip wondered aloud what truths were being buried. Was the truth too painful to bear—or too shameful to admit? Setting the paper aside, he told Anna, "Maybe one day my children will learn the real story."

He wasn't alone. Across the country, young Americans were beginning to question everything they'd been taught.

They weren't looking for easy answers anymore—they were searching for truth, no matter how uncomfortable.

As 1963 faded into 1964, the media landscape was evolving too. Evening newscasts expanded from fifteen to thirty minutes. With televisions now in over 90% of American homes, the screen had become the nation's communal hearth. Images—more than words—were now shaping public perception.

Whether it was the bloodied faces of Freedom Riders or the ecstatic screams of Beatles fans, the medium was redefining how stories were told—and how they were understood.

Those televised images ignited arguments between parents and children. Around dinner tables and across lunch counters, the generational divide deepened. For Phillip and his peers, asking *"Why can't I grow my hair like Paul McCartney?"* was about more than a haircut. It marked the beginning of a cultural and ideological shift.

The same television that had united the nation in grief after Kennedy's death was now chronicling its fragmentation.

Each evening, the family gathered around their console TV, the soft glow casting shadows on their faces as *The*

CBS Evening News with Walter Cronkite brought the civil rights struggle into their home. Black-and-white images of peaceful protestors marching through Southern streets— holding signs that read *"I AM A MAN"* and *"EQUAL RIGHTS NOW"*—became as routine as dinner.

Phillip watched with growing unease. The police dogs, the fire hoses, the billy clubs—it was horrifying. His stomach twisted with each new broadcast. Though his school and neighborhood were almost entirely white, he couldn't fathom the hatred directed at Black Americans.

"I thought this was all settled after the Civil War," he said one night.

Anna replied gently, "No, son. That was just the beginning. They still have a long way to go. The March on Washington was a start..." She paused. "But I'm not sure they're helping their cause by rioting and looting their own cities."

Jim added only one comment: "Nobody cared about their skin color when they were bleeding on the battlefield in World War II."

On July 2, 1964, President Johnson signed the Civil Rights Act in a televised ceremony from the East Room of the White House, using seventy-five pens that would later be given as keepsakes. The Phillips family watched as Johnson's Texas drawl gave voice to a new law that outlawed discrimination based on race, color, religion, sex, or national origin.

Phillip understood the significance. He had watched the struggle unfold night after night. Still, with a maturity beyond his years, he knew a signature on a piece of paper wouldn't immediately erase centuries of injustice.

"This is just the beginning, isn't it?" he asked his father later that evening, as they sat on the porch. The thick summer air buzzed with fireflies and distant fireworks.

Jim nodded, pipe in hand. "Laws can change overnight, son. Hearts and minds take longer."

Phillip pondered those words. The Civil Rights Act marked a monumental moment—but the fight wasn't over. Not even close. The coming months would bring more unrest, more reckoning, and more hard questions about the kind of country America wanted to be—and the kind of man Phillip was becoming in this new and uncertain world.

Chapter 3: The Summer of Innocence and Upheaval

Even with the passage of the Civil Rights Act, things didn't seem to improve. In Iowa, national news felt distant from the daily life of the community, yet it dominated headlines—and dinner conversations, which occasionally turned heated enough that someone was asked to leave the table.

After watching coverage of the Watts Riots—a six-day series of violent confrontations between Los Angeles police and residents of the predominantly African American neighborhoods of South-Central L.A.—Raymond muttered, "I don't understand why those Niggers are burning down their own neighborhood."

The table fell into a heavy silence. Anna finally broke it, her voice steady but resolute as she addressed Raymond's transgression.

"Raymond," she said, her gaze unwavering, "in this family, we do not use language that strips people of their humanity. You're Irish—how would you feel being dismissed as a Paddy or a Mick? Your question deserves to be discussed, but the language you chose undermines everything we claim to believe in."

The rest of dinner passed in silence. Afterward, the boys retreated to their room to finish homework.

On March 7, 1965, the nation watched in horror as Alabama state troopers brutally attacked roughly 600 peaceful civil rights marchers crossing the Edmund Pettus Bridge in Selma.

The television broadcast showed tear gas and Billy clubs used to strike demonstrators in the head until they lay unconscious. The chaos and hatred were palpable, coming through the television screen. Anna, eyes locked on the screen, murmured, "My God, why did you take John away from us?"

She believed that if the President hadn't been killed, things would be different under his leadership. The assault— quickly dubbed "Bloody Sunday"—sparked nationwide outrage and galvanized support for the Voting Rights Act of 1965. Yet, despite this legislative milestone, marchers and their supporters knew they were still far from the "promised land" Dr. King so often spoke of.

Phillip, meanwhile, had discovered two new passions to rival his love of baseball: music and girls.

In the '60s, rock and roll exploded with a new sound that divided generations. On Sunday nights, the family gathered around the new color TV to watch *Disney*, *Bonanza*, and *The Ed Sullivan Show*. The boys were excited—tonight's *Ed Sullivan* guest was a secret they hadn't shared, anticipating their father's reaction.

Midway through the show, Sullivan made the announcement: "Back for their third appearance—I give you The Beatles!"

Dad's face twisted in confusion. He'd heard their music, always from behind a slammed door as Arthur and Phillip played 45s too loud. But now he was seeing them. He watched for 30 seconds, then stood up, crossed the room, and switched off the TV.

"Oh my God! Don't they get haircuts in England anymore? And couldn't they have gone to the bathroom before jumping around like that? I've heard better sounds from an alley cat in a garbage can. Now, off to bed. You've got school tomorrow."

Phillip turned to Mom, hoping for backup. But she only

smirked, head down, continuing to knit.

Raymond wasn't into music much, aside from The Supremes. But Art and Phillip devoured it: The Beach Boys, The Rolling Stones, The Dave Clark Five, Jefferson Airplane, The Mamas and the Papas—and, of course, The Beatles.

Anna loved The Beach Boys and The Mamas and the Papas. When Jim wasn't home, she'd tell the boys to "turn it up" and would often be caught dancing in the kitchen.

Music was Anna's escape, a portal back to her carefree days before the war. The harmonies of "California Dreamin'" transported her from their modest Midwestern home to the sunlit California beach she'd seen during Jim's training days.

Phillip and Arthur were now attending Evans Junior High. With the first school dance approaching, Phillip was nervous about asking a girl to go with him. He'd been watching a redheaded girl named Annie in homeroom.

Curious but unsure, he turned to Raymond for advice.

"Ask if she'd be okay with you walking her home and carrying her books," Raymond suggested. "Gives you time to talk. See if you have anything in common."

Friday afternoon, heart pounding, Phillip approached Annie as she organized her books.

"Hi, Annie," he said, his voice a bit higher than intended.

She turned, surprised, then smiled. "Oh, hey Phillip."

"I was wondering... would you be okay if I walked you home? I could carry your books."

She blinked. "Don't you live on Appanoose? I'm on Ransom—that's way out of your way."

Phillip nodded, disappointed, and turned to leave.

"But," she added, "if you don't mind the inconvenience, I'd like that very much."

Phillip struggled to play it cool, but inside he was screaming, *Touchdown!* He smiled. "Great. I'll meet you after the final bell."

They walked, talked music and school, and by the time they reached her house, she'd agreed to go with him to the Barn Yard Hop. Before going inside, Annie smiled and kissed him on the cheek.

Phillip didn't walk home—he floated. Until he reached the front door.

"Where have you been?" Anna asked. "You're thirty minutes late."

"I walked a girl from class home," Phillip said sheepishly.

"Was she hurt? Why couldn't she walk herself?"

Phillip blushed. "No… Ray thought it'd be a good way to see if she might like me. I asked her to the school dance."

Anna's sternness faded slightly. "Next time, tell someone—like Art—so I don't worry. Do you like her?"

"I think I do. And I think she likes me—she kissed me on the cheek."

Anna turned away, hiding her smile. "Go wash up. Your dad will be home soon, and you've got a physical with Dr. Brodie for football. You still planning to try out?"

Phillip nodded.

"Then you might want to wash off that cheek," she teased.

Later, as the boys teased Phillip about his romantic success, Jim brought out paperwork for Raymond.

"You're turning eighteen in December," he said. "It's time to register for the draft."

Raymond's face fell. "Is this because of Vietnam?"

The war was everywhere on the news. What had once been "advisory" had turned into a full deployment. Bombing campaigns, combat troops, escalating conflict—it was now impossible to ignore.

Anna shot Jim a look across the table. It was the familiar, silent language of long marriages. Her eyes urged him to change the subject and wrap up dinner so they could begin the nightly dish debate: who would wash, who would dry, who would put away.

Later, gathered around the television, Anna sat apart, lost in thought. The news showed American soldiers trudging through the jungle, protestors chanting in growing crowds. She was beginning to accept what she had feared: the Navy might be Raymond's best option. Jim had waited too long during World War II and had ended up drafted. She couldn't help but wonder—would this war take all her boys?

As the school year ended, Phillip's thoughts returned to baseball. He had joined the Babe Ruth League and been placed on the same team as Art: the John Deere Tigers. Phillip was a catcher, the same position he had played since convincing his father to let him join Little League.

His idol was Yogi Berra of the New York Yankees. Phillip had become a skilled, vocal catcher, making the all-star team last season—a spot he would keep through his years on the American Legion team.

Catching was more than a position to Phillip—it was a leadership role. He saw the entire field. He called plays, shifted defenders, and even talked to the batters.

In one game, with Art pitching, Phillip became increasingly frustrated. The umpire wasn't calling the corners. After a couple of missed strikes, he called time and walked to the mound.

Watching from the stands, Anna nudged Jim. "Oh boy. This won't be good."

Phillip saw the irritation on Art's face. "Next pitch," he said, "fastball, just above your left shoulder."

"Why?" Art asked.

"Because I'm your catcher," Phillip said. "Just throw it."

As Phillip got into his crouch and put down one finger for a fastball, he felt the umpire lean in over his shoulder. Art threw the pitch—right on target—which sailed past Phillip and hit the umpire square in the mask.

Phillip quickly turned and said, in a voice loud enough for the whole field to hear, "Did you see that one?"

Many in the crowd erupted in laughter, even some in the opposite dugout. After some confusion, the umpire promptly ejected him from the game.

As Phillip walked toward the bench, he turned to Art and said, "Nice pitch."

After the game, his coach confronted him in the parking lot.

"What were you thinking?" the coach asked.

The assistant coach met Phillip at the dugout entrance. "Well, I hope that was worth it," he said.

As Phillip was getting out of his gear, he looked at the coach and said, "It was. I thought I needed to protect my pitcher. He had been squeezing him throughout the entire game, and I figured it was my job to do something about it."

The coach tried to keep a straight face and said, "Maybe next time try something more subtle. We need you in the game."

Anna looked at Jim and said, "Remember a couple of years back he couldn't even get the ball to second without bouncing it?"

Jim nodded. "Now look at him—taking charge and being the captain on the team."

Two weeks later, Phillip had the same umpire. He extended his hand and said,
"I hope there aren't any hard feelings between us."

The umpire studied Phillip for a minute and said,
"How about you catch, and I'll call balls and strikes today?"

Phillip said, "Yes, sir." But as he walked back to his dugout, he mumbled to himself, "My grandmother can see better than him."

This may have been Phillip's first ejection, but over the years he would play baseball, it wouldn't be his last.

Chapter 4: Embracing the Next Journey

In the fall of 1966, Phillip would join his brother, Art, at high school. This was a big move, and Phillip was a little apprehensive at first, because life at "the big house"—as everyone called it—was going to be a significant change from his years in elementary and junior high. The massive brick building loomed at the top of the hill, its shadow stretching across the parking lot like a silent warning of what lay ahead.

The first challenge was the three-day sophomore hazing ritual that every student experienced, dating back to when his mom attended high school. Anna had shared her own stories of the tradition, laughing as she recalled being made to recite the school fight song while hopping on one foot in the cafeteria.

"It's a rite of passage," she'd told Phillip with a nostalgic smile. "You'll look back and laugh someday, just like I do."

Hazing activities included shining shoes, carrying

someone's books, or singing a song when asked by an upperclassman—all part of the traditional high school welcome. On his first day, a senior girl with cascading blonde hair and a letterman's jacket stopped Phillip in the hallway.

"Sophomore?" she asked, one eyebrow raised.

Phillip nodded, his throat suddenly dry.

"Perfect. I need someone to carry my books to chemistry." She thrust a stack of textbooks into his arms that felt like they weighed as much as he did.

The hallways seemed impossibly long and crowded with unfamiliar faces—a sea of teenagers moving between classes. Navigating between rooms with only five minutes to spare added to his anxiety. Lockers slammed, echoing down the corridors like gunshots, and upperclassmen shouted greetings across the hall with a confidence Phillip could only envy.

Having Art already there, who had gone through his sophomore hazing the previous year, helped ease Phillip's concerns. The evening before his first day, Art sat on Phillip's bed, holding a hand-drawn map spread between them.

"Look," Art said, his finger tracing lines across the paper. "You've got English here on the second floor. Then you need to take the east stairwell—not the main one, that gets too crowded—to get to math on the third. If you hustle, you can make it with about thirty seconds to spare."

Art helped Phillip map out the quickest routes between classrooms and explained that these teachers were strict about tardiness. He also introduced Phillip to some of his friends, creating an instant social circle that made the transition less intimidating.

On that first lunch period, Art waved Phillip over to a table.

"Guys, this is my brother Phillip," Art announced. "Phillip, this is the crew."

Despite his initial worries, Phillip soon discovered that high school offered exciting new opportunities—sports teams and new teammates, the freedom to choose some of his own classes, and a lot more girls to catch his eye.

Raymond had enlisted in the Navy Reserve as planned and was stationed in the Philippines, where he would complete his service requirements as an aviation ordnance man. His main job, as he told them in letters home, was to handle all aircraft ammunition. He would pack everything from guns and ammo to missiles and bombs onto helicopters and fighter jets. He moved weapons, lifted them, stored them, tracked them, and transferred them to neighboring ships.

He described the weight of responsibility he felt, knowing that one mistake could cost lives—not just in potential accidents, but by failing to ensure pilots had what they needed when they flew missions.

Anna was sad he was so far away from home but was also thankful he wasn't in Vietnam.

The letters home were sporadic at first, postmarked from Naval Base Subic Bay, the stamps exotic and colorful against the cream-colored envelopes. Raymond wrote of the oppressive heat that seemed to stick to his skin day and night, "like wearing a wet wool blanket you can never take off." He described the monsoon rains that turned dirt roads into rivers of mud within minutes, and the meticulous procedures they followed when handling ordnance.

"One mistake," he wrote, "and you might not get a chance to make another." His detailed descriptions painted pictures of a world so different from Ottumwa that it might as well have been another planet.

His handwriting, once loose and carefree, had tightened into something more precise—much like the man he was becoming. His letters now contained neat, measured sentences that marched across the paper in perfect formation. Anna noticed the change immediately.

As she had done with the letters she received from Jim during World War II, Anna kept each of Raymond's letters in a shoebox tucked away in her closet, simply marked *"Raymond."* Sometimes, when the house was quiet, she would take them out and reread them.

Phillip signed up for the sophomore football team, and even though he was small—just five-seven and about 140 pounds—he knew that being the fastest kid on the team would assure him a spot. The football pads engulfed his frame, making him look like a turtle carrying its house, but once he started running, nobody laughed.

Coach Shoemaker was skeptical at first, saying, "This isn't track and field, son." His doubt was plain on his face as he watched Phillip line up for drills. But over time, during practice and scrimmages, Phillip eased the coach's concerns.

On a particularly hot August afternoon, with the grass yellowing beneath their cleats and the air thick with humidity,

Phillip broke free during a running drill—gliding through the defense like they were standing still, all the way to the end zone.

Phillip overheard Coach Shoemaker telling another coach, "We might have something here. This kid's got wheels."

In one memorable game, Phillip was brought up to the Junior Varsity team, along with several other sophomores, to see how they'd perform against bigger, more experienced players. The opposing team, confident in their size advantage, hadn't counted on Phillip's speed.

He scored five touchdowns—one called back because the team had too many players on the field during an interception return. The game opened with Phillip running the kickoff back for a touchdown. He ended it with an interception, snatching the ball from its intended path like he knew where it would be all along, and taking it 75 yards for the score—his legs pumping like pistons as he crossed the goal line.

After the game, the team boarded the yellow school bus for the ride home with a 57–14 win. The windows fogged with excitement and the air filled with the smell of sweat, grass, and victory. Phillip sat in the back, accepting slaps on the shoulder, trying not to look too pleased with himself—knowing it was his teammates who had opened the holes and given him the chance to shine.

Anna and Jim attended the games when they could. Anna used to cringe whenever Phillip went into a pile and disappeared, only to suddenly burst out of it, running past everyone.

"I don't know whether to watch or cover my eyes," she'd confess to Jim, who would laugh and pat her hand reassuringly.

By the end of the season, no one questioned whether Phillip belonged on the field. Anna kept newspaper clippings from the *Ottumwa Courier* featuring his success, and Coach Shoemaker told Phillip, "You taught me something—never measure a player by his size, but by his heart."

It was time for Homecoming, the first big social event of the year. The whole town seemed to vibrate with anticipation. Decorations appeared in shop windows downtown, and spirit banners stretched across Main Street, proclaiming "Beat Central!" in bold letters.

There would be a parade through downtown, class floats, the varsity football game—and, of course, finding a date for the dance in the school gym.

The sophomore class had been working on their float for weeks: a papier-mâché bulldog (the school mascot) standing triumphantly over a fallen opponent. Phillip helped after practice, working alongside classmates and making new friends as they crafted something special.

Phillip wasn't shy, but he wasn't sure who might say yes if he asked. Annie, his crush from junior high, was going steady with someone else. It made him wistful for simpler times, when holding hands in the hallway had been the height of romance.

Now, Phillip had his eye on a particular cheerleader—Terry—but he couldn't help feeling she might be out of his league.

For three days, he rehearsed what he might say, practicing in front of his bedroom mirror.

"So, I was wondering if maybe you'd want to go to the dance with me? If you're not already going with someone, I mean."

But despite his hesitancy, he asked—and she said yes. The word fell from her lips so easily that he almost asked her to repeat it, sure he must have misheard.

These events came with certain requirements: buying a suit, getting a flower corsage, and posing for family pictures. Jim took Phillip downtown to Brody's Store for Men, where Mr. Brody helped him find just the right suit—a dark navy blue—along with a tie that complemented it perfectly.

The corsage was an arrangement of white roses with a hint of blue ribbon to match Terry's dress—information Art had obtained from Terry's best friend.

On the night of the dance, they posed for photos at each of their parents' houses for the obligatory snapshots. Anna fussed over them both, straightening Phillip's tie and exclaiming over Terry's dress, while Jim stood back with the camera, snapping pictures.

"You both look wonderful," Anna said, her eyes suspiciously bright with the kind of tears mothers shed at these milestones.

But beyond all the formalities, Terry and Phillip had a genuinely enjoyable first date. The gym had been transformed with streamers and balloons; the harsh overhead lights dimmed just enough to set the mood. A live band played many of the songs they'd listened to on their record player at home, and they danced until it was time to go.

Jim picked them up and drove Terry home. Phillip walked her to the door.

"I had a really good time," Terry told him, the porch light casting soft shadows across her face. "Really."

Then she kissed him—a brief, sweet touch of lips that left Phillip floating all the way home.
His first kiss.

That spring, Phillip joined the sophomore track team—a group that would go on to break several school records, including the 220 dash, quarter mile, and relay records in the 880 and mile medley. The cinder track became a second home. The rhythmic pounding of feet, the sharp scent of liniment and sweat, and the ever-present smell of towels that should've been washed weeks ago filled the locker room.

Art was on the varsity squad and a member of the record-setting 440 relay. The brothers pushed each other in practice, working side-by-side on their starts out of the blocks.

Several sophomores, including Phillip, earned their first varsity letters, while Art received his second. That year, both boys added letter jackets to their Christmas lists, eager to show off their athletic accomplishments.

When Christmas morning arrived, they found identical boxes under the tree, wrapped in festive paper. Inside were the coveted red-and-white jackets. Anna had sewn the letters onto the chest and their class year onto the leather sleeves.

They tried them on immediately, posing in front of the bathroom mirror and sliding their hands into the pockets with the casual coolness they'd practiced.

"Now they'll never be able to tell you apart," Jim joked—though the brothers couldn't have looked more different. Art had the height and broad shoulders, while Phillip was leaner and quicker on his feet.

Anna took photos, of course, capturing the moment when her boys stood side by side in their matching jackets.

The only real problem Phillip had at school was getting to class on time. Apparently, no matter how fast he was on the track or football field, he still couldn't seem to make it from his girlfriend's class to his own within the five-minute passing period.

It wasn't that he couldn't physically cover the distance—his legs could get him across the building in under five minutes if the hallways were clear. But they never were. And then there was Terry, waiting outside her classroom with that smile that made him forget things like clocks and tardy slips.

The result of his time management failures often landed him in after-school detention, where the clock on the wall ticked away slowly, each minute stretching into an hour. He and Mr. Geith, the Vice Principal, would come to know each other well over the next three years, as Phillip racked up more than his fair share of detention slips.

Mr. Geith was a study in contradictions—stern-faced, with a voice that could freeze a student mid-stride. And he was considerably taller than Phillip.

Another issue Phillip seemed to have was his tendency to be somewhat of a prankster or class clown, which didn't always work out in his favor. He couldn't help himself—there was something about making people laugh that filled him with a satisfaction like nothing else. The sound of laughter rippling through a classroom was worth almost any punishment.

Case in point: one spring day during his sophomore English class on the third floor, as everyone got settled, the windows were open to catch a breeze that carried the scent of freshly cut grass and the distant hum of a lawnmower. Mrs. Solisberry was at the blackboard, her back to the class, writing the day's assignment in chalk that squeaked occasionally, sending shivers down spines.

Phillip placed some of his books on the windowsill, balancing them precariously. When Mrs. Solisberry wasn't looking, he nudged them with his elbow, sending them tumbling three stories to the school grounds below.

"Mrs. Solisberry," Phillip called out, his face a mask of innocent concern, "my books just fell out the window."

She turned and peered over her glasses with the weary look of someone who had taught teenagers long enough to expect mischief in every "accident."

"Well, I suppose you'll need to retrieve them. Take a hall pass."

He was given permission and the pass, and off he went. But by the time Phillip finally returned to class—after a stop at the water fountain, a short conversation with another student, and a leisurely stroll through the mostly empty halls—the bell was ringing, signifying the end of the day.

Seeing the satisfied smile on Phillip's face as he re-entered the classroom just as other students were packing up, Mrs. Solisberry realized she'd been pranked. The books, slightly battered but intact, were clutched in his arms.

"Phillip," she said, her voice carrying over the shuffle of departing students, "I believe you and I have some unfinished business."

She assigned him forty minutes of detention after school, to be served over two days. It equaled the amount of time he had missed in class—a kind of poetic justice not lost on him. He considered it a fair trade for the freedom he'd gained and the story he now had to tell.

High school turned out to be less stressful than Phillip had feared. He made new friends and took part in many of the typical high school activities: dances at the YMCA, the corral, and weekend live band performances at the Ottumwa Coliseum.

The Coliseum was a place Jim and Anna used to go before the war to listen to big bands like Tommy Dorsey and Glenn Miller. When Phillip mentioned going to a dance there, Jim's eyes lit up with memories.

"Your mother could dance all night," he told Phillip. "Light as a feather in my arms—even in those heels she insisted on wearing."

Anna blushed at the memory and swatted Jim's arm playfully. "Those shoes pinched something terrible, but I wasn't about to let anyone know that."

The boys also hung out at George's Pizza, where the air was thick with the smell of tomato sauce and melted cheese. The jukebox in the corner played everything from The Doors to The Supremes. They "scooped the loop"—driving endlessly around the main streets of town, windows down to catch the evening breeze, nodding at other cars filled with classmates doing the exact same thing.

For the first time, Phillip experienced a kind of independence his parents had trusted him with—freedom shaped by responsibility. He still had chores and a curfew, and rules to follow, but the reins were looser now, a quiet acknowledgment of his growing maturity.

His close friends, Rodney and Max, already had their driver's licenses and a '57 Chevy that meant they no longer needed rides from their parents. The car was a beauty—turquoise and white, with tail fins that looked like they could lift off. The inside was worn but clean, and the radio was always tuned to KYOA.

The Chevy became their constant companion, carrying them to football games, drive-in movies, and weekend trips to Lake Wapello, where they'd swim until their skin wrinkled, then lie on the shore, letting the sun dry them as they talked about girls, sports, and what came after high school.

Weekends were always full. Phillip realized that with all the new friends he'd made, his first year flew by faster than any school year before. Friday nights meant football or basketball games, followed by burgers at the Canteen, where the counters were packed with classmates reliving the night's highlights.

Phillip felt there was something unique about the Class of '69. Maybe it was the music that seemed written just for them, or the changes sweeping across the country that both frightened and inspired them. Or maybe it was just the experience of growing up together in a town where everyone knew everyone—and probably your parents, too.

They developed a closeness that would last long past their school years—a bond like Phillip had never experienced before. Inside jokes that needed only a word or a glance to send them into fits of laughter, shared secrets kept with the solemnity of blood oaths, and the unspoken understanding that this feeling, this friendship—was something to be treasured.

School was out for the summer, which meant it was time for baseball, hanging out with friends, and finding a part-time job. The days stretched ahead like an open road, full of possibility and free of homework or early morning alarms. But with that freedom came a new responsibility.

Jim and Anna had made it clear to both boys: with freedom came the expectation of earning their own spending money.
"You're old enough now," Jim said over dinner one evening, "to understand that nothing in this world comes free."

Anna nodded in agreement. "Your father and I will always provide what you need, but the extras—those are up to you now."

She suggested they check the want ads in the *Ottumwa Courier*. Spread across the kitchen table, the newspaper soon held a handful of circled listings—possibilities the brothers considered over breakfast.

Art found work at Safeway, his friendly demeanor winning over elderly customers who needed help getting groceries to their cars.

Phillip landed a job downtown at Brown's Shoe Fit Company. Mr. Otis, the owner, was looking for part-time help and was willing to work around Phillip's school activities.

Phillip had to catch the bus into town since Anna didn't drive and Jim was at work. The commute soon became a ritual—familiar faces each morning nodding in recognition, the town gradually waking as shops opened and the streets filled with people.

The job paid $2.25 an hour. Working 25 hours a week during the summer, Phillip could clear almost $50—a solid wage for a high schooler.

He needed to save some of his earnings, but part went to bus fare and lunch—usually at the Canteen, where the best loose-meat sandwich in town was served on a soft white bun with crisp pickles and a chocolate malt so thick the straw stood straight up. Across the street at Dupee's Bakery, he'd splurge on a Texas donut—a ring of fried dough as big as his hand, glazed and sticky sweet. No matter how carefully he ate it, there always seemed to be sugar on his shirt.

Don Otis was a good boss. He understood that a high school kid had priorities beyond work. He was flexible with scheduling, always making room for track meets or school events.

"School comes first," he insisted whenever Phillip needed time off. "The shoes will wait."

But there was one day a year when everyone was

expected to show up: Crazy Days.

And boy, was that the right name for it.

Crazy Days was a town-wide sidewalk sale that transformed Main Street into a carnival of commerce— clothing racks lined the sidewalks, tables of discounted goods spilled from every storefront, and shoppers moved in a constant stream, hunting for bargains.

Phillip arrived at 7:30 a.m. to help set up displays— rolling racks of shoe boxes out onto the sidewalk and organizing them by size and style. By noon, the summer heat was in full force, and the crowds were thick, hunting for deals and shade in equal measure.

After the parade—a procession of local bands, classic cars, and the Crazy Days Queen waving from a convertible—the pace picked up. The store buzzed with energy. Women tried on four or five pairs of shoes at once. Children squirmed while their mothers checked for "room to grow."

Phillip worked straight through until 5:30. By the end of the day, his feet ached, his back was sore, and his shirt clung to him with sweat. He caught the bus home, eager for dinner and a well-earned rest.

It was his first Crazy Days, but not his last. He walked away with a new appreciation for what his father meant about earning your way.

That evening, Phillip collapsed onto the couch, shoes kicked off and feet propped on the coffee table—a liberty Anna allowed only on special occasions. He couldn't help but feel a deep sense of accomplishment.

The money in his pocket was his—earned through his own effort and responsibility.

Life was good, and for Phillip and Art—brothers just fourteen months apart in age and only a year apart in school—it was even better. More than siblings, they were best friends. They had so much in common, including a shared group of friends, that disagreements about where to go or what to do were rare. They had their squabbles, of course—all siblings do—but those brief flare-ups passed quickly, leaving no lasting damage.

One afternoon, as they sat around the dining table, Jim made an announcement.

"I think it's time you had your own wheels. Your lives are getting too busy, and I can't haul you everywhere anymore."

The boys exchanged glances—a silent flash of disbelief

and excitement. A car of their own?

"But," Jim continued, raising a cautionary finger, "it comes with responsibility. Your mother and I aren't made of money. And neither are you."

If they wanted a car, they would need to share it—and more importantly, they would need to help pay for it. Between their part-time jobs, they could afford a modest payment and split the cost of insurance. Shared ownership was no hardship compared to the freedom a car would bring.

That Saturday morning, Jim took them to the Post Office Credit Union—a small brick building that smelled faintly of coffee. The loan officer, Mr. Hamilton, had known the family for years and smiled as Jim explained the purpose of their visit.

"These boys are responsible," Jim said, placing a hand on each son's shoulder. "They've got jobs, and they understand what it means to make payments on time."

Mr. Hamilton nodded, his pen already moving across the forms. "I've known you boys since you were in diapers," he said without looking up. "If Jim says you're good for it, that's good enough for me."

Loan approved—with Jim as cosigner—the next stop

was Glover Ford, the dealership where Jim had bought every car he owned since coming back from the Army. It felt like a wonderland of chrome and possibility. The rows of vehicles shimmered in the summer sun like soldiers in formation.

Mr. Gustafson came out to greet them.

"Afternoon, Jim," he said. "Shopping for yourself or is it the boys this time?"

Jim explained what they were looking for and how much they could afford. The salesman nodded knowingly.

"I think I've got just the thing."

He led them past the sparkling new models—well out of their price range—to the back lot, where the used cars sat in less precise rows but held no less promise of adventure.

That's where they found it: a 1960 Ford Falcon, four-door, beige. The paint was faded in places, the upholstery worn, but when Art turned the key, the engine purred like a satisfied cat.

"She's not much to look at," Mr. Gustafson admitted, patting the hood fondly, "but she belonged to Frank Guest, and you know how he is about his cars."

The price was right—$650. Their loan would cover the cost and the first six months of insurance. It was a car. *Their* car. The first real possession that would be theirs alone.

Jim had made one thing clear: ownership meant responsibility. There would be no bailouts if they missed payments. And if their car broke down, they wouldn't be borrowing the family one.

"She's all yours," Jim said, handing them the keys with the formality of passing a torch. "Take care of her, and she'll take care of you."

Art, being the oldest, drove it home while Phillip rode shotgun. Jim followed behind. Art felt every bump in the road, every turn of the wheel, as if the Falcon were made of glass. She may have been a little rough around the edges, but to them, she was perfect.

When schedules conflicted and neither wanted to give up the car, they flipped a coin—a ritual treated with sacred solemnity. The outcome was final. That was the deal, and both understood the alternative was no car at all.

Sometimes they still had to rely on friends for rides or catch the hourly bus that slowly crawled through town, but those were small inconveniences in a much bigger picture.

The Falcon became more than transportation. It was their freedom, their escape, their sanctuary—where they could talk about the future or just enjoy the ride. They went to drive-in movies, dated without needing a parent behind the wheel, and felt what it truly meant to be teenagers.

The world opened up in every direction, roads branching out toward discovery and independence.

Life was good. The car made it better—expanding their world and offering the kind of freedom that came with responsibility and trust. The future could wait. For now, they had friends, family, a Falcon, and an open road ahead.

Chapter 5: Echoes of Change

In the fall of 1967, it was time to head back to school. Art was beginning his senior year, and Phillip would be starting his junior year, which promised more academic requirements and commitments than ever before.

It was time for fall football to begin. The school had brought in new coaching staff, which meant Phillip would once again have to prove that his smaller stature was not a limiting factor in his ability to contribute to the team's success. The two-a-day practices in the August heat and humidity were taking their toll on everyone. Players throughout the team experienced heat-related injuries, cramps, and dry heaves.

After the second week of practice, the new head coach pulled Phillip aside, concerned about Phillip's ability to stay healthy through a grueling season. He figured Phillip would be best suited for kickoff and punt returns, at least for now. Phillip protested vigorously, pointing to his success as a sophomore and the impressive record the team had achieved the previous year. His voice rose as he argued that this year was no different from before.

"Yes, the players are bigger," he accepted. "But I haven't lost any speed. I can still outrun anyone on the field." His eyes flashed with determination as he insisted that he could not only maintain but also exceed his previous performance.

The coach acknowledged Phillip's speed, but he still wasn't convinced Phillip would be able to handle the physical contact that came with Varsity football.

Phillip had a decision to make. If he were to believe the coach, he would need to talk with Coach Warren, who had approached him about joining the cross-country team, one of which his brother Art was already a part. Jim discussed Phillip's future in football with him. He suggested that, given his love for baseball and track, it might be better to avoid any injuries by playing football and making the switch.

"You have nothing to prove to anyone. And why would you want to play for someone who doesn't believe in your talent? Just follow your gut and do what it is telling you," said Jim.

At the next practice, Phillip informed the football coach that he was going to run for Coach Warren and wished him well in the upcoming season. The football coach hadn't anticipated Phillip quitting the team. He tried to convince him to stay, saying, "I know you can help us; I just don't know where that is right now."

Phillip thought to himself, 'I've already shown you.' Instead, he thanked him. He told the coach that he thought it best not to get hurt, as the coach believed, and go with the sports he had a real passion for.

The cross-country team had two exceptionally talented long-distance runners, Chickering and Potter. Phillip, who typically ran 3 to 5 miles a few times a week to maintain his conditioning and had never particularly enjoyed long-distance running, made a strategic decision. Despite his preference for sprinting, he realized he could best serve the team by running interference, positioning himself as a buffer between opposing competitors and his teammates. This would give these two extraordinary runners a tactical advantage, enhancing their chances of victory. Phillip was a sprinter, not a pacer. His mindset was to go as fast as he could for as long as he could until he crossed the finish line. But he would honor the commitment he had made to the team and Coach Warren and do his best. He would earn his second Varsity letter that year, one he wasn't sure he really earned.

Phillip's journey through his junior year proved challenging in ways he hadn't anticipated. He struggled to craft an academic schedule that would spark his intellectual curiosity while simultaneously fulfilling the graduation requirements for the following year. Each class selection felt like a strategic decision in a game where the rules kept changing.

He had initially signed up for algebra. But Phillip wasn't grasping the concept of using letters to complete a math problem, and he couldn't see how this was going to help him when he got out of school. So, embodying the class clown persona that had become his trademark, Phillip couldn't resist the opportunity when his teacher solemnly declared, "Pi r squared." With perfect comedic timing, he raised his hand and announced to the entire class, "Well, where I come from, pie is round!" The classroom erupted in laughter, but his teacher was far from amused.

The following day, Phillip found himself in the counselor's office, where they promptly withdrew him from algebra and, ironically, placed him in advanced math instead.

Phillip's motivations for enduring high school were refreshingly uncomplicated: meeting his parents' expectations, excelling in sports, attracting girls, and savoring the carefree moments that defined teenage life in

America. While other students stressed over college applications and career paths, Phillip moved through the hallways with an easy confidence that came from knowing exactly what lay ahead.

He knew the path he was going to take. College wasn't in his plans. Neither did Phillip have the desire to go, nor could he afford it, as he knew his family couldn't help him financially. His plans were simple; join his brothers in the Navy when he was old enough to do so.

On September 15th, after turning 18, Arthur, like Raymond, flew down to Olathe Naval Air Station in Kansas, along with his best friend Tom Dawson, and enlisted in the Navy Reserves. They both would be going to basic training and A school once they graduated in June. Once their training was complete, they would be stationed wherever the Navy needed them most.

The family's television had become a window into a world of chaos, constantly broadcasting grainy footage from Vietnam's battle-scarred landscapes. Every evening at 6:30, they would gather and watch Walter Cronkite's grave voice recite the day's casualty figures with mechanical precision. The numbers were no longer abstract statistics but potential death sentences for boys they knew—neighbors, classmates, and soon, perhaps, family. The war had escalated dramatically in the past year, and now, over 500,000 American troops were deployed in Southeast Asia. For the brothers, military service wasn't just a family tradition—it was a duty they felt compelled to fulfill despite the risks they all knew existed.

Christmas break arrived with a special surprise— Raymond was granted leave and came home for the holidays. The family was complete again, if only for a short time. Raymond had changed; he was more serious, more focused. He didn't speak much about his experiences, but there was a new maturity in his eyes that wasn't there before.

"I'm not going to tell you not to join," Raymond said to Phillip as they sat on the front porch. His voice sounded deeper than Phillip remembered. "But listen to me on this." He turned to face his younger brother. "Choose a specialty that translates to civilian life. Electronics, communications, mechanics—something you can use after you're discharged." He paused, choosing his words carefully, "It won't be forever. And when it's done, you'll need skills that matter outside of the military life."

Phillip nodded solemnly, though, truthfully, his thoughts

had never ventured beyond the enlistment office. The future beyond service was a blank page he hadn't yet considered filling.

January brought with it more news of escalating conflict. The Tet Offensive was about to begin, though no one knew it yet. The Johnson administration continued to assure the American public that progress was being made and that there was 'light at the end of the tunnel.' But a growing sense of unease had begun growing within too many households.

Arthur, meanwhile, was counting down the days until graduation. He and Tom had already received their orders to report. Art had always been the serious one, methodical in his preparations. His approach to military service was no different.

One evening, the family gathered around the television as usual for the evening news. The reporter was discussing the growing anti-war movement on college campuses nationwide. Footage showed students burning draft cards and protesting with signs that read, "Hell no, we won't go!"

"I don't understand them," Arthur said quietly. "Don't they know someone has to go?"

Phillip looked at his brother, noticing for the first time the weight of responsibility Arthur carried. It wasn't just about following in their brother's footsteps anymore; it was about duty at a time when many were refusing to serve.

The protests grew louder and more frequent. The music was now adopting an anti-war message. Performers like Bob Dylan, Joan Baez, Phil Ochs, and Peter, Paul, and Mary became known for their protest songs.

Pressure was mounting on President Johnson as daily protesters stood outside the White House screaming, "Hey, Hey, LBJ, how many men did you kill today?" Those voices echoed in the president's head as he watched several newscasts each night from his residence.

With pressure mounting, not just from protesters but from members of his own party, President Johnson announced at the end of a speech that he would not run for reelection nor accept the nomination of the Democratic Party if offered.

As candidates scrambled to secure the Democratic Party's nomination, one person stood above the rest, capturing not just the hope for so many but an end to the turbulence that was seen every day.

Robert Kennedy hit the trail running, speaking of civil

rights, ending the war in Vietnam, and forging a new beginning. Phillip, perhaps because he was a Kennedy who spoke with a Boston accent, watched and cheered him on, to the displeasure of both his parents. However, Kennedy was gaining popularity among African Americans, anti-war activists, and independent voters. He was becoming a serious threat to the current Vice President, Hubert Humphrey.

Things changed as the announcement came over a news bulletin on April the 4th, 1968, that the Reverend Martin Luther King Jr. was shot to death as he stood on the balcony of the Lorraine Motel in Memphis, Tennessee. Moments before the fatal shot rang out at 6:01 PM, Robert Kennedy was supposed to address a mostly all-Black crowd in Indianapolis, Indiana. Many on his campaign wanted him to cancel this campaign, fearing violence. But Bobby refused. "They need to be comforted," he said, and he went.

Many in attendance had not heard about the assassination when Bobby delivered the news in the dark from the bed of a pickup truck. He told the crowd that Dr. King's death was tragic and we all had the right to be angry. But he urged all to respond with understanding and compassion rather than violence and anger, just like Dr. King would have wanted them to do.

After the boys had finished helping in the kitchen, they were seated in front of the television watching the Carol Burnett Show when the bulletin came across the screen. The regular program cut away to a somber news anchor, his face grave as he delivered the details.

Anna dropped her hands, glaring at the screen, and said, "Oh my God, when is this going to end?"

Everyone else just stared at the screen as if it was not real. Phillip's father, Jim, sat motionless in his recliner, holding his coffee mug and smoking his pipe, when he said, "I was afraid this would happen."

Art and Phillip got up and went to their bedrooms to listen to music, review their homework, and talk about their weekend plans.

The war in Vietnam had always seemed like a distant reality, something that flickered across television screens during the nightly news. That changed in April when Phillip learned that Johnny Link, the brother of a close friend from Walsh Catholic High School, had been killed in action.

Johnny wasn't physically imposing, but he possessed an unwavering determination to make his mark on the world. He had fought hard to be selected for the Green Berets, an elite special forces unit comprised of the military's finest soldiers. When accounts of Johnny's final day reached home, the truth of his heroism became undeniable.

In his last hours, Johnny had displayed extraordinary selflessness, repeatedly putting himself in harm's way to save his fellow soldiers. Despite sustaining multiple wounds, he managed to rescue seven men from certain death. His final act was shielding a fallen comrade with his own body, absorbing the fatal shot that would have claimed his life.

For his sacrifice, Johnny was posthumously awarded the Distinguished Service Cross—the second-highest medal for combat heroism—along with a Purple Heart. Many, including Phillip, believed Johnny deserved the Medal of Honor. But it was 1968, and Vietnam had become deeply controversial. Some suggested that the nation's leadership had decided they didn't need a hero, especially not a quiet Irish kid from a small town in Iowa.

Phillip visited the family at the Traul funeral home. He gave each family member a hug before approaching the glass-covered coffin. That visit would leave a lasting effect on Phillip, as it was the first time he had ever seen a dead person. He lay there, so peaceful in his military uniform, holding his green beret cover. Phillip knew there were thousands in the streets protesting not just this war but those who were carrying it out.

At home, Phillip looked at Anna and said, "They don't show this part."

"What part?" Anna asked, looking over at him.

"The funerals. The families. They show the protests and the soldiers, but not what I saw today."

Jim set his coffee down. "Nobody wants to see that, son."

"Maybe they should," Phillip replied, the image of the peaceful face beneath the glass cover still fresh in his mind. "Maybe they need to."

Phillip went on to say, "Maybe if everyone could see the sacrifices that are being made, they might change their mind and support our troops and not degrade them."

Anna carried her worry like a physical burden, her shoulders gradually bowing under its weight. She had already watched Raymond disappear into the vast military machine, his letters home becoming increasingly vague and sporadic. Soon, Arthur would follow, his bedroom becoming another shrine to absence. The prospect of eventually surrendering Phillip, her youngest, to the same uncertain fate made her hands tremble as she folded laundry or prepared dinner. Never once did she voice these fears—the McManus family valued their self-control above all—but her eyes betrayed her every time the television mentioned Khe Sanh or Da Nang, widening slightly with an ancestral terror known to mothers throughout history.

Chapter 6: The Day the Music Died Again

June 3rd was graduation day for Arthur. The ceremony was held at the large gym at Evans Junior High. Inside, the bleachers groaned under the weight of expectant parents, boisterous siblings, and proud grandparents who fanned themselves against the stifling heat of the late afternoon. As the ceremony dragged on through speeches about bright futures and boundless potential, Phillip's mind wandered through a slideshow of memories.

Phillip started recounting elaborate childhood pranks, argued good-naturedly about long-settled baseball disputes, and remembered arguing over music, girls, and car usage. He had to chuckle to himself when he recalled a weekend incident when Arthur had accidentally dropped a cherry bomb in Dawson's Volkswagen bug while it was full of friends. Luckily, Tom was able to pull over in time for everyone to get out before it exploded, leaving a cloud of smoke and a hole in the carpet on the car floor.

Art's family watched as he walked across the stage to

accept his diploma. He flipped his tassel and pumped his fist in the air, indicating that he had done it.

Phillip felt a surge of pride mixed with a strange sadness because in just a few weeks, Art, his lifelong friend, and brother, who he could talk to about anything without too much judgment, would be heading to the Navy. Art met up with Phillip after the ceremony and gave him the keys to their car. He told him that he didn't need the car tonight as he would be going out for their graduation party with friends. He said he wasn't sure what time the party might end. But he was almost certain he wouldn't be home in time for Phillip to go to school.

Jim walked in the door and saw Phillip sitting in his chair reading a book while listening to the Cubs, Anna's favorite team.

"How are they doing today?" he asked.

Phillip looked up at his dad and told him they were losing. He started to get up from his father's chair. Jim laughed and said, "I am glad to see some things aren't changing." Anna overheard the comment, giving Jim that look that told him to change the subject.

Jim picked up the paper and asked Anna how long it

was before dinner. She said he and Phillip could go wash up now because she was going to be putting it on the table in a few minutes.

"You're early tonight, what's up?" Anna asked. She wanted to watch the coverage of the Democratic primary tonight from California to see if Vice President Humphrey, who had gotten a late start in the primaries, could pass Senator Kennedy for the nomination.

"I don't know," said Jim, "that kid has a lot of momentum from the colored people, hippies, and young protesters."

"Don't their votes count like the older people?" Phillip interjected.

Jim ignored the question and reminded Phillip to go wash up and help his mom set the table for supper.

Anna had fixed Phillip's favorite meal, which she usually prepared on the day she and Jim got home from grocery shopping. Loose meat sandwiches with chips, onion dip, and milk.

"Thanks, Mom," Phillip said.

Anna told Phillip not to get used to it, explaining that it was fast and easy to clean up, and she wanted to relax and watch TV tonight rather than being stuck in the kitchen. Jim ate two sandwiches while Phillip devoured his usual four. It was a lot for a skinny kid who never seemed to gain any weight. Art was working late at the grocery store, so Anna reminded Phillip he might want to save some for his brother when he got home.

After supper was done and cleaned up, Anna took off her apron and sat down on the couch. Picking up her knitting, she asked Phillip to change the channel to WHO 13 to watch the coverage. Phillip got up, changed the channel, and adjusted the antenna.

It was after midnight when the results of the California primary were confirmed. Kennedy had emerged victorious, capturing 46% of the vote. At the same time, his closest rivals, Senator Eugene McCarthy and Vice President Hubert Humphrey, split the remainder of the ballots. The June 4th victory all but assured Kennedy of the Democratic nomination, bringing hope to a nation still reeling from the assassination of his brother and the escalating violence in Vietnam.

The ballroom of the Ambassador Hotel in Los Angeles hummed with excitement. Red, white, and blue balloons bobbed against the ceiling as campaign workers and supporters pressed forward to catch a glimpse of their candidate.

Senator Robert Kennedy approached the microphone, and his wife, Ethel, stood beside him with a broad smile.

"And now it's on to Chicago, and let's win there!" Kennedy declared, his Boston accent rising above the cheers as he referenced the upcoming Democratic convention.

Hands reached out to touch him as he waved to the adoring crowd, his hair falling across his forehead as he began his exit through the hotel kitchen. Hotel staff paused in their work, some reaching out to shake the Senator's hand.

Suddenly, shots rang out, and Senator Kennedy was lying on the floor from two gunshots from a .22 caliber pistol. He lay on the cold kitchen floor, blood pooling beneath his head where a bullet had entered behind his right ear. Despite the grievous injury, he remained conscious for a time, his eyes reflecting confusion and pain. His last words before he became unconscious were, "Don't lift me."

He was rushed to the Good Samaritan Hospital in Los Angeles, where he died the next day, June 6, 1968, at 1:44

a.m., almost 24 hours after he was shot. As the news blasted over the morning, Anna was once again taken back to that day in Dallas five years ago.

"That poor family," she whispered, her voice cracking. "How much pain does one family have to witness?"

She set her coffee down, unable to hold it because her hand was shaking so badly.

Phillip and Art had just woken up, and when they came out from their bedroom, rubbing the sleep out of their eyes, they once again saw their mom sitting with her head down, crying.

Both boys turned to the black and white footage, which showed the chaotic scene at the Ambassador Hotel, played on a loop as if forcing America to confront its violence over and over again. They saw Kennedy lying on the floor, blood staining his shirt, while people screamed and scrambled around him. They both didn't say a word. They just walked over to the couch and sat down, each taking their mom's hand while staring off into space.

After a few minutes, Anna stood up, and wiped away a tear. She reached for the knob on the TV set. "Can we please turn it off? I can't watch anymore," she told Phillip.

As the screen went dark, the room fell into silence, broken only by the sound of dishes Anna was stacking in the kitchen and the ticking of the cuckoo clock in the hallway.

Phillip needed to go someplace—anyplace—so Art handed him the keys and said, "Go. I'll stay with Mom."

He didn't need to explain; Art understood that look in his eyes, that desperate need to escape the suffocating grief that filled the small living room.

Phillip backed out of the driveway, tires squealing slightly against the pavement. He drove aimlessly through the streets, windows down, letting the wind whip through his hair. The 8-track played the music louder than usual—some Doors album Max had left in the car—the volume cranked up in a futile attempt to silence the noise in his head.

"What the hell!" Phillip shouted out the window as he slammed his fist against the steering wheel until his palm stung with pain. The physical sensation was almost a relief compared to the hollowness inside.

Phillip ended up at Wildwood Park, pulling the car into the nearly empty lot. He sat on a picnic table, staring across the park where children played.

"How do you just sit back and let this happen?" he

asked, looking up at the sky. Was he really talking to God? Phillip wasn't sure he even believed anymore. He reached into the car and found a crumpled pack of cigarettes someone had left behind.

Phillip only smoked on occasion, but he figured he needed one now. Time passed unnoticed as Phillip sat there, smoking until the sun started to set, casting long shadows across the park. Finally, Phillip slid off the picnic table, his body stiff from sitting for too long, and drove home. Phillip had no answers, just a feeling of defeat.

Once again, the nation would watch on television the process and funeral of another man who only wanted to make the world better for all.

The Kennedy family waited at the Good Samaritan Hospital for the post-mortem examination. The body was put into its coffin, and after a quiet Mass, the body of Senator Kennedy was placed aboard the plane sent by President Johnson to bring him back to the East Coast. Los Angeles added its name to the list of cities whose previous history has been defaced by acts of violence.

The plane touched down at John F. Kennedy International Airport in New York around 4:30 Eastern Standard Time. Kennedy's body was taken to New York for the funeral in St. Patrick's Cathedral.

Jim, Anna, Art, and Phillip sat in front of the TV watching the funeral. Finally, Teddy Kennedy, the last brother, walked up the steps to the pulpit to deliver his remarks. As he looked out into the crowd and said, "My brother need not be idealized, or enlarged in death beyond what he was in life; to be remembered simply as a good and decent man, who saw wrong and tried to right it, saw suffering and tried to heal it, saw war and tried to stop it.

Our future may lie beyond our vision, but it is not completely beyond our control. As he said many times, in many parts of this nation, to those he touched and who sought to touch him: 'Some men see things as they are and say why. I dream things that never were and say why not.'"

After the Mass, Robert's body was then taken by a special train to Washington DC, past enormous grieving crowds, who lined the tracks paying their respects and expressing, once again, their sadness.

Anna wiped the tears away as she observed the obvious grief of those watching the train go by, hoping to catch a brief look at his flag-draped coffin sitting inside a car that was still visible to the crowd.

Robert Kennedy was buried in the dead of the night, close to his brother John, in Arlington National Cemetery, marked with a simple white cross.

Phillip, who was sitting next to his mom, looked at her and said, "I think we need to stop asking questions that have no answer. And instead of asking 'why?' we should start asking why not."

That night, as Anna and Jim settled into bed, the weight of the day still hung in the air. The bedside lamp cast a soft, amber glow across their room.

"I'm worried about the boys," Jim said. "Art seems to be handling it okay, but Phillip—"

Anna replied, "Phillip takes everything to heart, always has."

Jim asked if Phillip had said anything when he came back. "He was gone a long time."

Anna said, "Not much. Phillip has been more affected by these events than Art. JFK, Vietnam, and now this. But I was encouraged by something in his expression today."

"How so?" Jim asked, reaching over to take her hand.

"These tragedies, as horrible as they are, they're

shaping him," Anna said, her voice growing more certain as she spoke. "It's like watching him find his moral compass, Jim. He's asking the big questions—the ones about justice and meaning. The ones that help a young man find the path he'll take in life."

Jim was quiet for a moment, considering her words. "You might be right," he finally conceded. "When I was his age, it was Pearl Harbor that changed everything. Made me realize there were things worth fighting for."

Anna squeezed his hand. "I just hope he doesn't get too lost in his anger. That he finds a way to channel it into something good."

"Phillip will find his way," Jim said. "These moments, as terrible as they are, help to show us who we are. Or, in the boys' case, who they will become."

Chapter 7: A Senior Year in the Shadows of Change

On July 8, 1968, the family loaded up the car to take Art to the Des Moines airport so he could go to his Basic Training in Olathe. The weather was hot and humid, and since Jim's car didn't have air conditioning, everyone rolled down the windows and hoped Jim would drive fast enough to get some air inside. It also helped the smoke from Anna's cigarettes and Jim's pipe to escape.

Art would be flying down with Dawson and was excited to get the adventure started. Phillip asked his dad if they had time to stop in Des Moines and get a tenderloin from Pokey's.

"You buying?" asked Art with a grin.

"Not a problem, bro. I just got paid, and it will probably be the last one you're going to get for a while."

Anna said there was plenty of time. "The airport is small, and all that has to be done is to show his orders, drop off his duffel bag, and make the short walk to the gate."

As they were getting out of the car, they saw the Dawsons pull into the parking lot. Apparently, Tom had the same idea.

Mrs. Dawson rushed over to Anna, clutching a handkerchief already damp with tears. "I told myself I wouldn't do this," she said, dabbing at her eyes. "But here I am, falling apart before we even get inside."

Anna, having already done this with Raymond, squeezed her friend's shoulder. "We'll get through it together. Come on, let's go in and eat."

The 1968 Democratic National Convention was held August 26–29 at the International Amphitheatre in Chicago, Illinois. Phillip had little interest, but Anna enjoyed watching the coverage. She knew this convention wouldn't be like any she had ever seen before.

Chicago's Mayor Richard Daley had no intention of letting his city or the convention be overrun by protesters.

Anti-war demonstrations around the city grew, with some turning violent and many being crushed by police.

These protesters were angry, not just about the war, but

since Senator Kennedy was killed, they had no voice to represent them. They seemed to believe that the older generation didn't care or share their vision of tomorrow.

"Turn that up," Anna said, leaning forward in their living room. The television showed chaotic scenes from downtown Chicago.

Phillip sighed but reached for the volume knob. "I don't see why you're so invested in this mess."

The footage cut to scenes of chaos. Police in riot gear were advancing on the crowds. Some protesters were throwing objects, while others stood with arms raised, chanting, "The whole world is watching!"

Then came the shocking images that would define the convention: police officers wielding batons, striking not just protesters but journalists and bystanders, blood on the pavement, and young people being dragged away.

"My God!" Anna whispered, her hand covering her mouth.

Inside the convention hall, the discord was just as pronounced. The division wasn't just on the streets—it had penetrated the Democratic Party itself—the old guard versus the new.

As the night wore on, Vice President Hubert Humphrey would secure the nomination, but at what cost? The Democratic Party was fractured.

"They're going to lose in November," Phillip said, breaking his long silence.

"How do you figure that?" Jim asked.

"With the Republicans trying Nixon again, Humphrey for the Democrats, and that nut job from Alabama, Governor George Wallace, he will take the southern Democrats' votes. I don't see how Humphrey can win."

Anna acknowledged the difficulties but remained hopeful nonetheless. This would be Phillip's first time voting, as he would turn 18 in October. He knew he would vote for Humphrey. But he wasn't enthusiastic about his vote because he didn't see any change in any of his options.

Phillip started his senior year on September 3rd. He had lost all interest in playing sports and had come to the realization that going to the games would be more fun than playing in them. His desire was to make the most of his last year. Maybe get a few more hours at Brown's and spend more time just hanging out with his friends and classmates.

Phillip signed up for only the classes needed for

graduation. By doing this, he could be out by 1:40 every day, so he could go down to the Mission pool hall or just hang out downtown. The early dismissal gave him a sense of freedom his classmates wouldn't enjoy until summer.

The Mission pool hall had become something of an afternoon hangout over the past year, where friends could gather, play a few games of nine ball, and chill. The mustiness of the aging building, the smell of stale cigarettes, as well as the glare of the lights over the pool tables, greeted you when you walked in. Phillip was okay at pool, but knew better than to challenge Fisher, who would make a quick game of it if you did. And, of course, this early freedom was contingent on his ability to avoid detention.

Phillip had one more baseball game of his baseball career. He played for the OB Nelson Post #3 American Legion team. The last stop for organized baseball was in Ottumwa. It was one team made up of the best players, aged 16 to 18, who still wanted to play. Coach Harsch wanted Phillip on the team for his speed and his ability to steal bases, including home twice last year. He had convinced Phillip that he would best be suited for second base, utilizing his speed and his ability to get to ground balls. Phillip was okay with the move. Just being on the team was enough, and he figured his body could use the break from the beating it often took being behind the plate.

Tonight's game was a rematch with the Dubuque County American Legion Baseball team. Phillip made the drive over to the field that was located behind Wildwood School. As Phillip was warming up, he thought about the last time these two teams met. Losing 9 to 3. Phillip went 0 for 3, walking once and stealing one base. He was hoping for a better outcome tonight.

The field had been prepared for tonight's game. The air smelled of freshly mowed grass. The white chalk lines perfectly marked the foul lines, and the hum of the lights echoed softly as they were coming on.

"Play ball!" the umpire yelled, and the game got underway. It was a better game than the last encounter, with Phillip's team leading by one. It was the top of the seventh, with Dubuque County having runners on first and second and no outs. Coach Harsch yelled out to Phillip to move towards second to try to hold the runner on. As the pitch was delivered, both runners took off. The batter hit a line drive towards the middle. Phillip moved to his right, snagging the ball out of the air, stepped on second, and then tagged the runner, trying to get back to first.

Everyone, including the umpires, froze for a minute. It was an inning-ending triple play. Rare as they are, this was an extremely rare play because a single fielder recorded all three outs of an inning without any assists from teammates.

When Phillip got to the bench, there were slaps on the back, and Coach rubbed Phillip's head and said, "Now do you understand why I moved you?"

The OB Nelson team got their revenge by winning the game 6-3. Phillip didn't have a much better day at the plate, going 1 for 3 and striking out twice, but he had executed a triple play. Jim and Anna weren't at the game but heard all about it from Phillip when he got home. Jim even confirmed it the next day when he read all about it in the local sports page and when he stopped in the legion to have a beer.

School was going well for Phillip. Unlike many of his classmates, he wasn't fixated on grades and college applications. With his extended curfew, he found himself genuinely enjoying his senior year in ways he hadn't anticipated. The pressure that seemed to weigh down so many of his friends—SAT scores, college essays, class rankings—barely registered with him. He had his own path figured out, so he could take one day at a time.

The one area where Phillip lacked confidence was in

asking girls to go steady. He was popular for his quick wit, pranks, his success on the track, and the talent he displayed on the baseball diamond. But he didn't think most of the young ladies who caught his eye would be interested in anything beyond a couple of casual dates. Looking in the mirror each morning, Phillip didn't see himself as particularly handsome or cute. When it came to dating, he tended to "stay in his lane," asking out girls he thought might actually say yes and avoiding rejection.

He was comfortable with this arrangement, even as his friends paired off into couples. It made things less complicated as he could hang out with everyone without the baggage from past relationships interfering.

There was, however, one exception: a cheerleader who had a laugh that seemed to bubble up from somewhere genuine inside her. And a personality that made her easy to be around. She and Phillip had developed an easy friendship, and he didn't want to jeopardize that.

So, Phillip was content meeting up with the gang at the Southside Pizza Hut. They would split a few pizzas after dances at the coliseum, everyone talking over each other about the day's events or who had danced with whom. In these moments, with his friends laughing, Phillip felt perfectly at peace.

Besides, this was his senior year, and everyone would be going their separate ways soon enough—scattered to different colleges, jobs, marriages, or military service. He didn't need the drama of saying goodbye to a girlfriend when that time came.

Phillip learned he liked the taste of beer, even if it was Grain Belt or some off-the-wall brand no one had ever heard of. Rodney and Max had found a man who lived along the Des Moines River who didn't ask for ID but charged double the cost. The boys pooled their money from summer jobs, thinking the markup was just the price of being underage.

On the weekends, if the weather permitted, everyone would go out to someone's farm, where they would build a fire, play music on their boom box, and sit around, enjoying a few cold ones and each other's company.

Often, thinking they were safe being out on the farm, the music would get too loud, and everyone had to scurry when they saw the lights from the Sheriff's car coming down the long dirt road. They'd quickly throw the cans in the back of a pickup, kick dirt over the fire, and scatter.

One night, they got caught, not by the sheriff but by the

farmer. There was no time to run, so they stood their ground.

He looked around with his flashlight and said to Phillip, "Aren't you Jim McManus' boy?"

Phillip nodded yes, and the farmer, still looking around, said, "Turn that music down, and make sure this fire's out proper before you leave. My cows can't sleep with all this racket."

Phillip nodded sheepishly. "Yes, sir."

Mr. Franklin rolled down his window with one last request. "I don't want to see any evidence that you were here when I come back out in the morning."

After he left, they sat in stunned silence for a moment before erupting into relieved laughter. They turned down the music, but the night felt somehow better, not worse, for the interruption. Apparently, Mr. Franklin was young once and had recalled his youthful days. For Phillip, he wasn't so relieved. He was hoping what happened here wouldn't spread beyond this point because Mr. Franklin lived on his dad's mail route.

A few weeks after Phillip had turned 18, he and his dad were sitting in the living room watching the Bears. Jim got up during a commercial and went into the kitchen. When he returned, he had two cold beers in his hand.

"Here," he said to Phillip. Phillip looked confused as he reached for it.

Jim snickered and said, "I was told you enjoy a cold beer on the weekend."

Busted!

Phillip started to explain himself when Jim interrupted him."If you need a beer, have it here and not out on someone's farm."

That was a deal Phillip could live with.

Chapter 8: The Greatest Prank Ever

January 1969 arrived with Richard Nixon's inauguration, promising an end to a war that seemed to have no end. As Nixon spoke of "peace with honor," kids were wearing embroidered bell-bottoms and tie-dye shirts.

Hair was getting longer, skirts shorter. At the high school, there was even a test to ensure the girls' skirts met dress code: they had to kneel, and if the hem didn't touch the floor, it was deemed too short. The girls had a workaround. They'd hike their skirts at the waist to get the desired length and pull them down to regulation if questioned.

On January 24, Phillip drove to the Ottumwa airport. Once a Naval Air Station built during World War II, it had trained pilots, including a young Richard Nixon. The Navy had abandoned it in 1947, and the city had taken ownership.

Though six miles outside town, it was a popular destination for skating on a large wooden floor that had been built over an old pool used in the war. It was also the regional hub for Ozark Airlines.

Phillip, like his brothers before him, was flying to Olathe, Kansas, to join the Navy Reserves. He sat with Master Chief Smith, also the fire chief, and Petty Officer Phil Pain, a family friend who worked with Phillip's dad, Jim, at the post office. Soon, a C-47 Skytrain, an old WWII-era transport, rolled up to the tarmac.

Crew members helped them board. Phillip, clutching his bag, felt both nervous and excited. It was his first flight and the unknown ahead thrilled him to no end. As the aircraft taxied, he maneuvered to one of the few windows. The engines roared. The nose lifted, and they were airborne. He looked down, watching his hometown shrink into a miniature model below.

Inside the uninsulated cabin, it grew cold quickly. The men wore pea coats and stocking caps; Phillip pulled up the hood of his civilian jacket. Chief Smith said something with a smile, but it was hard to hear anything over the noise. The men played poker, pulled out flasks, and settled in for the trip.

When they landed, they hustled to the barracks, got their bedding, and headed to the enlisted men's club. Phillip followed Petty Officer Pain like a shadow. Phil helped him get settled and then asked, "Want a beer?"

"I'm only 18," Phillip said.

Phil clapped him on the shoulder. "Here, if you're old enough to serve, you're old enough to have a beer."

The weekend was packed. It started with breakfast at 6 a.m.—the biggest meal Phillip had ever eaten—followed by military testing to determine his placement. Then he received his uniforms: dress blues, whites, two sets of dungarees with a ball cap, and best of all, a pea coat and a navy-blue stocking cap. He felt like a real sailor.

The rest of the time was filled with basic training until Sunday, when they boarded the C-47 for the return trip. Snow was falling, and Phillip grew nervous. Pain noticed and grabbed his sleeve.
"Don't worry, this plane could fly through a hurricane. A little snow won't hurt it."

The flight home was bumpier. Each time the plane jolted, Phillip gripped his seat.

"Want a shot?" Chief offered.

"No thanks. I'm good," Phillip replied.

Back in Ottumwa, the familiar aircraft felt less

intimidating. Phil reminded him to keep an eye on the mail for orders about the next month's trip, flight times, uniforms, and training.

"Be on time. The Navy don't wait."

As Phillip headed to his car, Chief Smith called out, "See you next month, kid!"

Phillip fingered his Navy ID card as he drove home, proud to be following in his brothers' footsteps. He couldn't wait for next month.

April brought warmer weather and louder protests. This generation wasn't just opposing the war; they were redefining everything. Psychedelic music, marijuana, bras burned in protest, free love; all signals to their elders that they were forging a new path.

Ottumwa had its first war protest, and many of Phillip's classmates participated. Phillip didn't join them; he still believed in the war's purpose. But he stood outside Brown's Shoe Fit and watched. "Hell no, we won't go!" and "Peace now!" echoed through Main Street as protesters marched, carrying signs and homemade coffins.

Phillip's jaw tightened as he saw familiar faces, classmates he'd known for years. Some knew his brothers were serving, yet they marched. His fists clenched. Would they mock him too, if they knew he'd joined the Reserves?

He turned and went back into the store. Don looked up and, seeing Phillip's frustration, said gently, "You don't have to agree with them. But wearing the uniform means you understand they have the right to protest. Sometimes you'll hear things you hate, but that's what makes this country better; everyone has a voice."

Phillip nodded and turned to help a customer, an older woman who'd also been watching the protest.

"Disgraceful, isn't it?" she said.

He ignored the comment and focused on helping her.

Later, Phillip changed into his dress whites upstairs. He was off to Olathe again. When he came down, Helen exclaimed, "My goodness, Phillip! You look like you just stepped out of a recruiting poster."

Don nodded in agreement. Phillip stood a little taller, proud in the uniform that now meant something more than fabric and thread.

"You take care," Helen called as he left. "And don't let those kids bother you; they're just confused."

With only a few weeks left of school, Phillip began thinking about prom. He had the credits to graduate, and prom was the last big event. Becky Yates had recently broken up with her boyfriend, and they'd always been good friends.

Maybe it didn't need to be a date, just a fun night with no pressure.

Phillip asked Anna for advice.

"Just ask her," she said with a knowing smile.

Jim, lowering his newspaper, added, "You've got a 50/50 chance. You feel lucky?"

The next day at lunch, Phillip sat beside Becky. "Are you going to prom?"

"I don't know. I haven't been asked yet." She smiled. "Are you asking me?"

"Well... yes, I am."

"Then yes, I'm going. With you." She nudged his shoulder with a grin. Phillip smiled, relieved; he had a date.

On the last day for seniors, Phillip was determined to pull off one final prank—the best ever. He spread the word: bring an alarm clock to school. Before first period, everyone was to stop in the cafeteria, where he and a few friends would set each clock to go off at 9:30 a.m., then hide them in lockers throughout the building.

With nearly 600 seniors, even a third participating would cause chaos.

At 9:30 a.m., as classes were in session, the symphony of alarms exploded. Laughter erupted in every classroom. Teachers tried to regain order, but the moment belonged to the students.

A voice interrupted the buzz in Phillip's English class, "Pardon the interruption, but is Phillip in class today?"

"Yes, he is."

"Please send him to the vice principal's office."

As Phillip walked the halls, he wondered how many hours of detention this would cost. But it was the last day. What could they really do?

Mr. Gieth stood waiting.

"Sit down," he said, sternly.

"I can't imagine any other senior causing this much chaos today. You do know I don't have to let you graduate, right?"

"Sir, do you really want me back next year?"

Mr. Gieth paused.

"You've got a point." He leaned back. "Any more surprises?"

"No, sir."

"Good. Go back to class."

As Phillip turned to leave, Mr. Gieth added,
"In all my years, that was the best prank I've ever seen." He shook his head. "God help the Navy."

Phillip grinned wide as he walked back to class. Mission accomplished.

Graduation week arrived. Practice was held in the gym, the air buzzing with anticipation. At Sunday's baccalaureate service, families gathered for a quiet, reflective ceremony.

Then came Monday, June 2. It was the day of graduation. The gym was packed. Behind the stage hung the class motto: **"Success and honor we combine—we're the class of '69."**

The guest speaker ran with it, oblivious to the double meaning that had made it so popular among students.

Phillip tried to focus through the heat and speeches. Growing tired, he leaned over to Steve Mullinix.

"Wake me when they get to our row."

Then, his name was called. Phillip stood, walked across the stage, and accepted his diploma. He turned and waved as Jim and Anna clapped, beaming with pride, and a growing sense of an emptying nest.

After the ceremony, he returned his cap and gown and picked up his official diploma.

Back home, the family hosted a celebration with pizza, soda, and congratulations. Anna's parents, Craig and Mary, and her brother Art were there. Phillip's friends stopped by before the big party at the Ottumwa Country Club.

At 7:00 p.m., it was time to leave. Anna told him to enjoy his night. Jim gave a word of caution: "The cops will be out tonight. Be smart."

Phillip wasn't sure when he'd be home. He had to be at work by 8:30 the next morning, but he was ready.

The party at the Country Club was in full swing. Food, music, dancing, games, everything a graduation celebration should be. By 1:00 a.m., it was winding down, but Max,

Rodney, and a few others weren't ready to go home. They ended up at a small café across from Vaughn's Chevrolet, eating and laughing until a food fight ended their night.

At 4:30 a.m., Phillip finally returned home, caught a quick nap, cleaned up, and went to work.

When he walked in the back door at Brown's, Don asked, "Didn't you graduate last night?"

"Yeah," Phillip said. "Just got home in time to come here."

Don smiled.

"You're not gonna be much help today. Go pick out any piece of Samsonite luggage you want—and go home."

Phillip picked out a suitcase he could use for his travels and headed home for some much-needed sleep.

As he drifted off, the whirlwind of the last 24 hours replayed in his mind—the ceremony, the celebration, the milestone.
One chapter closed.
A new one, already unfolding.

Chapter 9: One Small Step

Summer was here, and Phillip was working every day and banking his money. He had sent a couple of letters off to Raymond and Art, asking for any information they might want to share about basic training. Each gave examples based on their own experience, but there were a few common threads they agreed on: keep a low profile, don't talk unless talked to, the longer they don't know your name, the better, and don't volunteer unless you know what you're volunteering for. Art said to choose your friends carefully, and Raymond said not to take it personally when the drill instructor is in your face yelling; he's trying to see if he can rattle you. Don't let him, because it will only get worse.

The Fourth of July was always a big celebration at the McManus household. You see, Anna was born on the Fourth in 1920, and she and Jim were married on the same day in 1941—Anna's 21st birthday. Anna's dad told her, right before he walked her down the aisle, "Well, looks like you've gained and lost your independence on the same day."

The day would include grilling hamburgers, chilling watermelon in an old wash tub, lots of bottled sodas and beer on ice, and of course, hand-cranked homemade vanilla ice cream that everyone took a turn cranking, a treat everyone enjoyed in the evening while watching fireworks. Phillip loved ice cream, and because he always ate it so fast, he would have to stop due to brain freeze. Jim noticed and started laughing, telling Phillip, "I guess even at your age you haven't figured out ice cream needs to be eaten slowly."

Late that month, the family gathered in the living room to watch the first human landing on the Moon, which occurred on July 20, 1969, as part of the Apollo 11 mission. Astronauts Neil Armstrong and Buzz Aldrin landed the Lunar Module *Eagle* smoothly, and upon touchdown, they stated: The Eagle has landed.

Every man and woman who was in the space center broke out in cheers. Neil Armstrong at 02:56 GMT on July 21, 1969, stepped out of the capsule down the steps and onto the surface of the moon. He said, "One small step for man, one giant leap for mankind." He planted the American flag and became the first person to step foot on the Moon's surface. Jim, Anna, and Phillip took delight in watching his playful movements as he bounced around, the weight of his boots the only thing keeping him from floating into space. With amazed disbelief, Phillip had a big smile on his face.

"They've completed the dream President Kennedy spoke about when he delivered his first State of the Union in 1961. He said, 'We choose to go to the Moon... not because they are easy, but because they are hard.'"

Jim added, "This is an example of what we can do once we put our minds to it."

Anna replied, "Maybe they should use that same can-do spirit and end this damn war!"

As August dragged on, still hot and thick with humidity like a wet sponge, Phillip sat in his bedroom, going over the list of items he would need to take to boot camp. With some help from his dad, he packed everything into his duffel bag. He was careful not to wrinkle any of the clothes Anna had just finished ironing for him.

They walked out of the bedroom just as Max and Rodney pulled into the driveway. After talking for a while, they asked if it was okay to head down to Pizza Hut for one last large sausage pizza. Jim and Anna said to go ahead, but reminded them, "Tomorrow is going to be a long day."

Phillip understood and said he'd be home in a couple of hours.

It was Saturday, August 16th, and the house was

buzzing with activity. At 6:30 a.m., Anna was already up fixing breakfast for Phillip with all his favorite foods: pancakes, bacon, eggs sunny side up, coffee, and milk.

Phillip helped his mom clean up after breakfast, thanking her for the meal.

"You go sit with your father, I got this," Anna said.

Phillip replied, "No, I might need the experience when I get KP duty."

They worked side by side, sharing small talk, Anna pausing occasionally to wipe her brow with her apron, until everything was done.

Both joined Jim in the living room. Phillip went through everything he had packed, making sure he hadn't forgotten anything. Jim sat quietly, smoking his pipe and looking out the window, probably recalling the day he left for boot camp during World War II. Anna picked up her knitting and worked on a scarf for her dad's upcoming birthday.

Jim spoke up and asked Phillip if he knew what he would be doing in the Navy.

Phillip looked over and said they told him he could choose between air traffic control, like Art, meteorology, or becoming a hospital corpsman.

"Now how in the hell did they think a shoe salesman would make a good corpsman?" Jim laughed, recalling a story about a guy named Henry from Camp Dodge who had asked the same question. He told Phillip what he had told Henry years ago: "Well, apparently the Navy saw something you didn't. Don't worry, with training I'm sure you'll make a great doc if that's what you choose."

The cuckoo clock chimed 10:00 as Jim said, "We probably need to get going, especially if we plan on stopping somewhere to eat." So they loaded up Jim's 1967 Mercury Monterey and pulled out of the driveway.

"Hey Dad, I know it wasn't that long ago that we ate, but could we stop at the canteen for a couple of burgers?" Phillip asked.

"Oh my God, do you have a tapeworm?" Anna asked.

Phillip laughed, saying no, but it would be nice to have one more for the road.

Jim pulled up near Hoffman Drug, and they walked down the alley. They took a seat at the counter and placed their order. Phillip asked for one with mustard and ketchup, and Jim ordered one with everything. Anna said she was still full from breakfast and just ordered coffee.

As they were eating, one of Phillip's friends from school, Calvin James, came in and sat next to them. He noticed Phillip was in his dress whites and asked if today was the day he was heading to the Navy.

Phillip, with a mouthful, nodded carefully so as not to spill anything on his uniform.

They reminisced about the time Calvin had given Phillip a puppy from a litter his dog had, and the story Phillip made up to keep it.

Anna said, "You didn't fool us. If that dog was out in the snow, wouldn't you have thought his fur might be wet?"

They all laughed as Phillip admitted he hadn't fooled anyone. "Well, thankfully, you love puppies as much as I did," he said.

It was time to go, so Phillip said goodbye and offered to pick up the bill.

The lady behind the counter said, "No, you're not. You've been in here plenty of times, and today this meal is on us. Now you go, be safe, and come back in when you get home."

Phillip thanked her and headed out the door, the bell ringing one more time. As they walked back to the car, Phillip waved goodbye to Calvin and wished him luck at college as he was heading to the University of Iowa to be a Hawkeye.

The drive to Des Moines seemed shorter than usual. Maybe it was because Phillip's mind was racing with thoughts of what was to come.

Golden cornfields stretched endlessly on either side of Highway 163, a sight so familiar, yet suddenly precious. The radio played softly in the background, *In the Year 2525* by Zager and Evans, the futuristic lyrics taking on new meaning as Phillip contemplated his own uncertain future.

The family passed a billboard advertising Grain Belt beer, its colors faded by the relentless Iowa sun. Just beyond it stood another sign, newer and starker: *Support Our Boys in Vietnam*, with an American flag painted in the corner. The war hung over everything these days, protests on college campuses, debates at barbershops, somber announcements on the evening news.

"You nervous?" Jim asked, glancing over his shoulder at Phillip.

"A little," Phillip admitted, fidgeting as he stared out the window.

Anna turned to look at him. "Your Grandpa would be so proud of you boys. You know he served in the Army during WWI and the Navy in WWII. He always said it was a way to pay your debt for the freedom you had and pay it forward to help the next generation."

Phillip nodded, adding that he missed Grandpa Craig, who had passed away in June from emphysema.

"I will always remember his gentle quietness that made you feel safe," Phillip said, "when you were sitting on the front porch swing gazing into the sky."

It was early afternoon when they arrived at the airport. Phillip stepped up to the counter, presented his ID and orders, and handed over his duffel bag. The agent placed it on the conveyor belt and said, "Gate 3."

Phillip turned and rejoined Anna and Jim as they made their way through the terminal. Outside the window sat an American Airlines plane being prepped for departure. It would be Phillip's first time flying on a commercial jet.

Soon, the boarding call came over the loudspeaker.

"Well, I guess this is it," Phillip said.

Anna's eyes were already filling with tears. She turned away, not wanting to upset her son who had enough on his mind.

Jim leaned in. "Remember what Art and Raymond told you. And what I said too: keep your head down, do what they say, and before you know it, boot camp will be over."

Anna hugged Phillip tightly, holding him a little longer than usual. Her shoulders trembled slightly against him.

"Write as soon as you can," she whispered.

Jim extended his hand formally at first, then pulled Phillip into a hug. "I'm proud of you, son." His voice caught on the last word, and Phillip felt it settle deep in his chest. Praise from Jim McManus was rare, making it a treasure.

Phillip gave one final wave. "I'll see you both soon. Don't worry about me."

"It's our job to worry," Anna said, dabbing at her eyes with a handkerchief.

Phillip boarded the plane and found his seat by the window. He fastened his seatbelt and glanced up at the signs: *Fasten Seatbelt* and *No Smoking*. Soon, a man and woman took the seats beside him. They exchanged polite smiles, but no words.

The plane lifted off. As soon as the wheels retracted, the no smoking light turned off, and the cabin filled with cigarette smoke, making Phillip cough.

A memory surfaced: sitting on the porch swing at ten years old, listening to Grandpa Craig talk about the Pacific. Craig never mentioned combat. He spoke of camaraderie, the vast ocean, and strange ports that felt like other worlds. Phillip hoped to see those places himself.

Eventually, the man beside him turned. "Where you headed, sailor?"

"Boot camp," Phillip replied.

"Good luck. Just take it one day at a time. You'll get through it."

"Thanks. Did you serve?"

"Yeah—two years in Korea. Marines."

Phillip nodded, then asked, "Mind if I bum a smoke?"

The man handed him one along with a lighter. Phillip took a drag and exhaled slowly, handing back the lighter. "Thanks."

He turned back to the window. The clouds rolled past like smoke, and below, Iowa's farmlands stretched in perfect squares, a quilt of green and gold.

The flight attendant came over the intercom. "Ladies and gentlemen, we'll be arriving in Kansas City soon. Please fasten your seatbelts and stow your tray tables. We'll be coming through to collect trash."

The plane banked, lining up for descent. Phillip watched the buildings below rise into view. The wheels touched down with a squeal, and the plane slowed to a crawl.

At the gate, passengers filed out. Phillip thanked the couple and stepped into the terminal. Signs overhead directed him to baggage claim, where he waited by the carousel. Several duffel bags circled. He checked each tag until he found his.

Slinging it over his shoulder, he scanned for transport. A blue bus idled outside with *U.S. Navy* markings and "Olathe" printed on the overhead sign. Diesel fumes hung heavy in the humid August air.

Phillip took a deep breath, walked to the bus, and handed the driver his orders.

The driver nodded. "Climb aboard."

And with that, Phillip took the first step into his new life.

There were several other passengers on the bus, most in uniform, others in civilian clothing. They waited for the remaining riders to arrive, and once everyone was on board, the bus driver closed the door, saying it would take about 40 minutes to get to the air station.

"Sit back, relax, smoke if you want; you'll be there soon."

Phillip looked out the window, watching the landscape go by, when the guy sitting next to him said, "Do you want a smoke?"

Phillip turned and said, "What?"

The guy replied, "You want a smoke? My name is David, and I figured we're both heading to boot camp."

Phillip took a cigarette, introduced himself, and confirmed he was also heading to basic training. David asked where he was from, saying he was from Saint Louis. Phillip said Iowa, knowing he wouldn't recognize the name Ottumwa.

"So, are you a Cardinals fan or Cubs?"

"Cubs," Phillip replied.

"Cardinals or Bears?"

"Bears."

David laughed. "Well, we don't have that in common, but maybe we can still be friends."

Phillip remembered Art's advice about choosing your friends carefully, so he was polite but reserved in the conversation as they drove to the air station.

Finally, they pulled through the gates, and the bus came to a stop in front of a large brick building with the tallest flagpole Phillip had ever seen. As he got off the bus and walked to the doors, he looked up to see the American flag waving in the wind, as if it were saying, *Welcome aboard.*

Phillip was directed to a processing area where several other recruits were already sitting on worn wooden benches, hunched over clipboards, filling out endless forms with names, dates, medical histories, next of kin. A petty officer in a uniform with creases sharp enough to cut paper approached him. The man's name tag read "WINTERS," and a faded tattoo peeked from beneath his sleeve, an anchor with a date Phillip couldn't quite make out.

"Name?"

"Phillip McManus, sir," Phillip replied, remembering to stand straight, shoulders back, chin level, just as Jim had demonstrated that morning in their living room.

The petty officer checked his list, pen tapping impatiently. His eyes flicked up for just a moment, assessing Phillip in one practiced glance.

"McManus... here you are. Take a seat over there. We'll be calling names for processing shortly."

Phillip jerked his head toward an empty bench.

"And for future reference, son, I'm not a 'sir.' I work for a living. I'm Petty Officer Winters."

"First time away from home?" a boy asked, his voice cracking slightly on *home.*

"Yeah," Phillip admitted. "How about you?"

"Nah, my folks moved around a lot. Dad's in construction. Always chasing the next big project. I lived in six different states before I turned twelve. My name is Eddie Myers, by the way."

"Phillip McManus."

They shook hands. Eddie's palm was sweaty, but his grip was firm. A small callus on his index finger suggested hours spent with a pencil or pen.

"Where you from, Phillip?" Eddie asked, lowering his voice

as a stern-faced officer walked by, clipboard held like a shield against the civilian world they were leaving behind.

"Small town called Ottumwa, in Iowa. And you?"

"Originally Chicago—South Side," Eddie replied.]

"But we've been in Cedar Rapids the last couple years."

Their conversation was cut short as a Chief Petty Officer entered the room. His face was deeply tanned except for pale skin around his eyes. The chief's ribbons and insignia told a story none of the recruits could yet read, but they recognized authority when they saw it.

"All right, listen up! When I call your name, you will answer 'here' and follow Petty Officer Daniels through that door. He'll take you over to your barracks."

A scattered chorus of "Yes, sir" followed. The chief said, "I can't hear you."

"YES, SIR!" the room responded in unison, the sudden volume making the windows seem to vibrate.

Phillip looked at Eddie again and wondered if he'd just made his first Navy friend. Eddie glanced at him and gave a slight nod, as if to say, *We're in this together.* Phillip nodded back.

The journey had begun.

Chapter 10 : Hell Weeks Begin

The training all sailors go through is a six-week program focused on physical and mental conditioning, basic military knowledge, and the transition from civilian life to military service. It emphasizes discipline, teamwork, and readiness for future Navy service. It hasn't changed much over the years, especially when it comes to discipline, except that the Navy no longer uses flogging as a form of punishment. They have come up with other unique disciplinary techniques to get the same results. Phillip and his fellow recruits would soon find out just how effective these methods could be.

Phillip, along with fifty other recruits, was marched over to their home for the next six weeks. As they entered the barracks, Phillip saw beds arranged in a row, with windows void of shades or curtains. Behind and to the side of each bed was a standing locker, and at the foot of each bed sat a wooden footlocker.

The Petty Officer led them to an area that had been set up for display. "Here is what your bunk will look like." He then opened the wall locker, where they saw uniforms hung in a specific order, shoes and boots arranged neatly, and on the shelf above, hats and a shaving kit organized with military precision.

"Take a good look, because this is how your locker will look," he instructed. He walked to the end of the bed, opened the footlocker, and said, "Pay attention to what you see, because this is how your tray will look."

The shoe polish brush was positioned in the upper left corner. Underwear and T-shirts were rolled and stacked down the right side, and socks were placed precisely in the middle.

"What you do in the bottom of the locker is your business. But understand, this is what yours will look like— no more, no less," the Petty Officer stated with finality, his tone leaving no room for questions.

That weekend, they were given a list of all the toiletry items they needed to purchase at the Navy Exchange. They received inoculations, many wincing as needles pierced their arms in assembly-line fashion. Their initial uniforms were issued, and they underwent their first military haircut, which they were expected to pay fifty cents for, to the barbers who seemed to enjoy shaving their heads. They received stencils so they could mark each article of clothing with their name to prevent loss. A handbook was distributed, explaining much

117

of what they would have to learn, including general orders, rank identification, and terms used to identify things like the bathroom ("head"), walls ("bulkhead"), floors ("deck"), and so on.

They were told Reveille would come at 05:30. They had 15 minutes to get up, get ready, and fall out, quickly finding a spot marked on the parade field where they would stand. There would be no talking, no smoking, and, just for tomorrow, they were to be in their dungarees with white caps.

Whatever time remained in the weekend was theirs; though "theirs" was a relative term. They had to get their gear stenciled, stowed away, and bunks made to specification. Writing a letter home was mandatory, with the Chief making this crystal clear: "I don't want any damn phone calls from your family. You will write home once a week. Is that understood?"

The recruits responded in unison, voices echoing off the barracks walls: "Yes, Chief!"

Each recruit was busy trying to get everything done, and there wasn't time to get to know one another. That would have to happen in the barracks before Taps and lights out at 21:30 hours (9:30 PM). Phillip worked on getting his name on each item and then stowing it away.

They would wear green boxer shorts, which Phillip thought strange since he was used to briefs. But his mind was racing with everything he needed to remember that Art and Raymond had told him about being a good sailor and not standing out to the DIs (drill instructors).

One sailor, sitting on his footlocker spit-shining his boots, looked up and, to no one in particular, said, "Enjoy it while you can, because tomorrow the shit hits the fan."

Phillip paused in the middle of stenciling his name on a pair of boxer shorts, wondering how this recruit knew so much. The guy looked no different from the rest of them. He had freshly shorn hair, nervous eyes, fingers working frantically to prepare for whatever waited for them at dawn.

Yet something in his tone suggested experience, or perhaps access to information the rest of them weren't privy to.

Around him, the barracks buzzed with subdued activity: the scrape of stencil brushes, the snap of sheets being pulled taut over mattresses, the occasional muttered curse when someone made a mistake they'd have to explain later. The smell of shoe polish and cleaning supplies hung in the air, mingling with the sweat from the August heat and the scent of rain drifting through the open windows.

Phillip returned to his task, but the sailor's words echoed in his mind. *Tomorrow.* Whatever "Hell Weeks" truly meant, he would find out soon enough.

Phillip walked into the head and realized there wasn't going to be much privacy. Toilets with wooden seats had nothing dividing them except for the toilet paper holders mounted on the wall. Two interior walls had six sinks on each side. At each end were showers with no curtains. Outside, there was a small grassy area designated for smoking. They would soon learn it was required to field-strip their cigarettes once finished.

David Turley was on Phillip's right, and Eddie Meyers had taken the bunk to his left. Phillip figured they had decided they were going to be friends. Well, for now, all he wanted to do was find the mess hall for dinner. He was starving, having eaten nothing since he left the canteen.

Phillip took one last look at his lockers to make sure everything was in order before sitting down to write a short note home, letting his parents know he had arrived safely, things were going well, and that he was staying busy. He gave them the particulars for writing back:

Name: Airman McManus, P. C.

Service Number: B863071

Company C, 2nd Platoon,

Recruitment Center, Olathe, Kansas 66061.

"Lights out!" someone shouted, and everyone stopped what they were doing and climbed into their racks, throwing off the green woolen blanket and slipping under freshly starched sheets. The windows were open, and in the distance, the soft rumble of thunder echoed as *Taps* tried to muffle its sound.

"Get some sleep, McManus. I think tomorrow's going to be an entertaining day," Turley said, chuckling out loud.

At 0530 on the dot, the lights in the barracks blazed on as someone beat the hell out of a tin garbage can at the end of the room, yelling, "Get up, get ready, and I'll see you on the parade field in 15 minutes, and you don't want to be late!" Then the shadow disappeared into the darkness, walking out through the screen door and letting it slam behind him.

Phillip needed to pee and hustled to the bathroom, discovering 49 other guys with the same idea. There was no time now to do much except get dressed, lace up his boots, and get outside. The sun wasn't up yet, and the field was lit only by overhead streetlights. He found a spot and stood on it as Turley took the one next to him.

"I guess the definition of *morning* is different than mine," he whispered, then remembered: no talking.

The Chief, along with three Petty Officers, stood in front of them. One barked, "Attention!" Most had some general idea of that command from watching old military movies.

"Now look to your right and left, because from this day forward, that is who you should be standing next to.

"We are going to march from here over to the dining facility. Once there, you will go in, grab a tray, and the food the Navy wants you to eat will be placed on it. No talking in that line. You have 20 minutes to eat. When done, you will scrape your tray, stack it, and drop your silverware in the soapy water. Then you'll return to the parking lot. Smoke if you want, until you are called to fall in. Are there any questions?"

"No, Chief!" came the unified response.

"Left face!"

Obviously, some didn't know their left from their right, but eventually, they began the march over to the dining room with one of the Petty Officers calling out cadence: "Left, right, left, right. Get in step!"

They would spend hours during the next six weeks learning to march. Phillip found it similar to dancing, but you had to pay attention to the signal caller and not anticipate his next command. Others were so slow that the DI had to put a rock in their right hand and a leaf in their left until making those turns became natural, marching in formation and conducting crisp military movements.

As they filed into the dining facility, Phillip's stomach growled loudly. The smell of eggs, bacon, and coffee filled the air. Despite the institutional quality of the food, it looked like a feast to his hungry eyes. He grabbed his tray and moved quickly through the line, each server plopping portions onto his plate with mechanical efficiency.

Finding a seat at a long table, he began to eat quickly, knowing the clock was ticking. Around him, fifty other recruits did the same with their heads down, focused entirely on the task at hand.

Twenty minutes wasn't much time, especially when you were starving.

The real training hadn't even begun yet, but Phillip could already feel the Navy working its way into his system, regimented time, precise movements, and the clear understanding that from now on, his life would be dictated by orders and routines rather than personal choice. He finished his breakfast with five minutes to spare and followed the procedure for disposing of his tray.

After breakfast, the company was called to fall in. Once in place, they were called to attention as they waited for the national anthem to play. On the first note, the Petty Officer yelled, "Hand salute!" and everyone made their attempt to follow that order. They would later learn the proper stance, but for now, they looked at the flag being raised, squinting as the sun was directly in their eyes. The next command was "Two!"—whatever that meant—but there were enough in the platoon who understood they could drop their salute.

They returned to their barracks to make their beds, clean the room, and grab the materials they would need for the day: one number 2 pencil in your shirt pocket, your military ID, the book that was handed out earlier, and nothing else. Cigarettes were to be in your sock, if you smoked.

They spent the rest of the day either in a classroom or on the parade field learning to march as one. At one point, they were given a break.

"Smoke 'em if you got 'em," Petty Officer Dunkin said.

Phillip didn't have any smokes, so he borrowed one from Martinez. As they lit up, Dunkin started screaming.

"Where did you get the lighter, boy?" he shouted, getting in the face of one of the recruits. "I don't remember telling any of you that you could have a lighter, did I? Get down and give me fifty!"

Phillip technically didn't do anything wrong since he had borrowed both a cigarette and a light. But he didn't want to draw attention to himself, so he got down and started doing pushups, yelling out each rep. As Phillip was doing pushups, he realized it was a good lesson: do not assume anything and follow the instructions you've been given exactly.

But why give us a smoke break if you can't light them?

The question burned in his mind as his arms began to shake around pushup thirty-five.

The Petty Officer watched as they continued, finally announcing, "You can have a lighter, but it must be in the pack in your sock. Now get up, and next time pay attention to what you have been told. Do you understand?"

"Yes, Petty Officer!" came the unified response, voices slightly breathless from exertion.

Over the course of the next six weeks, they would all do enough pushups for a lifetime. The exercise became as routine as breathing; dropping for twenty-five here, fifty there, sometimes even more when someone made a particularly ignorant error, like calling a weapon a gun. Their arms grew stronger, their chests broader, but more importantly, their attention to detail sharpened.

With each pushup came a lesson that would serve them well in their Navy careers: never assume, follow orders precisely, pay attention to the details, work as one. The physical punishment wasn't just about discipline; it was about building the mental framework necessary for military service, where a small mistake could cost lives.

Phillip's hands callused over; he found himself completing sets that would have been impossible just weeks before. Sometimes, late at night as he lay in his rack staring at the ceiling, he would flex his hands and marvel at how quickly his body was changing. But the greater change was happening in his mind, a new awareness, a heightened sense of responsibility, and a growing understanding that in the Navy, you either learned these lessons or you recycled.

Going home wasn't an option.

By the third week, Phillip could recite the proper procedure for almost everything from memory, how to stow gear, how to address officers, the NATO phonetic alphabet, and even where to keep that troublesome lighter. The pushups continued, but they became less frequent as the recruits learned to listen, not anticipate orders, and execute them with precision.

"The Navy doesn't punish you," Petty Officer Dunkin told them one evening, as they stood, arms trembling from the day's physical training. "And these lessons will help when you're out there on a ship and someone's life depends on you following the procedure exactly as you were taught."

Phillip nodded. He was beginning to understand. Being in the Navy meant you had more to think about than yourself. You were on a team. Like football, nothing was going to work unless everyone was committed to doing their job to accomplish a common goal. In football, it was scoring a touchdown. In the Navy, the results of your commitment had much bigger consequences, either great reward or devastating failure.

Chapter 11 : Finding the Groove and Becoming Sailors

After three weeks of having their bunks tossed, lockers dumped, and doing pushups for not having their barracks ready for inspection, the platoon began understanding the meaning of teamwork. They utilized those who were best at certain tasks. For instance, those who were good at getting their racks tight inspected each one, making sure it met the standards. Others made sure the knot of the day was properly tied at the end of each rack. Lockers and footlockers were checked while others took a good look, trying to find all the pennies the DI had said they had put out to make sure they cleaned every square inch of the barracks.

Phillip was good at making a bed. He could get it so tight you could bounce a coin off of it. For the knots, not so much, as it was kind of like algebra back in school. He couldn't see any need for learning that since he was going to be a corpsman and not a boatswain's mate. But he kept that thought to himself. Complaining was a sure ticket to more pushups or, worse, being singled out for "special instruction."

Myers had become the unofficial expert on floor polishing. He'd grown up helping in his father's janitorial business and knew exactly how to make the linoleum shine like glass. Turley turned out to have an eagle eye for spotting those hidden pennies the DIs would place in obscure corners to test their thoroughness.

"Check under the radiator," Turley whispered one morning as they prepared for inspection. "I found two there yesterday."

Phillip nodded and bent down, finding not just one but three pennies tucked away where the shadow made them nearly invisible.

"Got 'em," he said with satisfaction.

By week four, inspections were no longer a problem, so they could move on to more intense training. Weapons, first aid, close order drills, night marches, and, of course, floating and swimming in the 100-meter pool.

The pool had been a source of dread for several recruits—especially Phillip. He could swim, but no matter how hard he tried, he never learned to float, his butt dragging him under. And now he had to jump in the water from the ten-meter platform in full uniform, surface, remove his pants while treading water, tie a knot in the legs, toss it over his head and float on them for fifteen minutes. Every time he would raise his arms down, he would go. Until one day, he watched others who held their legs up while they tossed their pants over. The last thing to graduate was to swim three hundred meters—the length one would have to swim from a sinking ship to avoid being pulled under with it.

The petty officer noticed that Turley was not a good swimmer. "Every sailor has got to learn to swim and survive in the water. The ocean doesn't care if you're a cook or a SEAL. You can't swim; it will take you under."

Turley looked at Phillip when he entered the water. "I can't do this," he whispered to Phillip. "I'm gonna wash out."

"You got this! Just keep swimming until they blow the whistle. You're not washing out."

It wasn't pretty, but with one stroke at a time, Turley noticed he was heading in the right direction. By the time he reached the 300-meter mark and surfaced, his breathing was labored, and his lungs burned from exhaustion. But he did it. Phillip gave him a hand as he climbed out of the pool. Others were still in the pool, struggling to tread water. Their arms were exhausted from push-ups, and they were now trying to stay afloat for the fifteen minutes required to move on. When the time ended, one by one, each sailor dragged himself from the poll's edge onto the wet deck. Every muscle ached, but they passed.

Only two would be returning for late-night remedial training. This exercise was not optional; you had to be able to survive in the water.

The weapons training was next and was Phillip's weak spot. He'd never been around guns before enlisting, and the weight of the rifle felt awkward in his hands. But just as he'd helped Myers, Turley—who'd grown up hunting, had helped him master the basics of handling, cleaning, and firing his weapon.

To qualify with the M14, a sailor had to fire 5 shots at a target that was 50 meters in front of them. They needed to put at least 3 of the 5 rounds on the target. The qualification required shooting from standing, kneeling, and prone positions. For Phillip, this wasn't just another test—it was his final chance to qualify before graduation.

Phillip approached the firing line. He could feel the weight of the 9.2-pound rifle in his hands, sweat beading on his forehead despite the cool breeze.

Phillip ran through the procedures in his mind: seat the rifle squarely on your shoulder, wrap the sling around your arm while holding the barrel firmly in your palm—not too tightly. Keep both eyes open for better depth perception. While breathing in, hold your breath and squeeze the trigger, not pulling it, which can cause you to jerk the rifle.

His instructor, Chief Myers, had drilled these steps into him for weeks.

The range officer's voice called out, "Shooters ready... commence fire."

Phillip looked down range, his heart rate slowing as he focused. The rounds cracked through the air as he fired. He hit 3 of 5 shots while standing, his hands steadier than they'd been during practice. Moving to kneeling, he felt more confident, connecting with 4 of 5 targets. Finally, in the prone position, the rifle steadied against his shoulder, and he achieved perfection—5 for 5.

After clearing his rifle and staffing it, Phillip stood with a mixture of relief and pride. Chief Myers approached while looking at his targets. "Qualified with a 12 out of 15. Not bad, sailor," he said, clapping Phillip on the shoulder.

Phillip smiled, looking toward both Turley and Myers,

132

giving them a thumbs up, signaling he was a go and, at the same time, a thank you for their help.

Close-order drills were becoming almost commonplace. There was something magical about moving in perfect unison with fifty other men, boots hitting the ground at exactly the same time, turns executed with precision. The rhythm had a hypnotic quality. For those brief periods, they weren't individuals anymore; they were one.

There were ten-mile hikes no matter the weather, the terrain, or even if the sun wasn't even up. They would march at 1500 hrs. or 0300 hrs. These were tests of endurance and will. They had to make a night march, get back to the barracks, and be ready for inspection in a few hours, often attending to boots that needed to be shinned to a glow.

"The platoon is getting good at this," Turley said. Phillip nodded. "Remember that first day when Martin warned us about what was to come? He had recycled but was now ready to graduate and move on."

The platoon had found its groove, transforming from individuals to becoming a team sharing the same goals. Taking advantage of each other's strengths while figuring out how to work together.

As Phillip lay in his rack thinking how, in just five weeks, the civilian habits were gone, replaced by military discipline. Just one more week, and it would be over. He had learned it wasn't just about shining shoes or making beds with hospital corners—it was about becoming something bigger than himself. 'One more week,' Phillip said to himself as he fell asleep with the gentle sound of taps playing in the distance.

With September here, the weather was cooling. And with the night breeze coming through the open windows, it was time to get under that old green woolly blanket they used to kick to the floor. Each sailor preferred keeping the windows open and pulling their blankets up to their necks instead of closing the windows. There was something soothing about letting the noises from outside in.

Finally, the graduation day arrived. The base was prepared for the guests, families, officers, and dignitaries who would be present. Every recruit put the final touches on their dress blues and shone their shoes to a high polish. In a ceremony the previous evening, each graduate had been awarded the National Defense Service Medal that they would proudly display on their uniforms.

Phillip had written home about the graduation but was certain his family wouldn't be able to make the four-hour drive. The recruits had marched and rehearsed to the music until they were almost exhausted. They knew when they passed in review in front of the Base Commander, Captain Johnathan "Jonny" Johanson, it had to be perfect. Phillip thought it was funny how they all had a sharper step when marching to John Philip Sousa's "Stars and Stripes Forever."

Master Chief Nelson, along with Petty Officer Duncan, came into the barracks and passed out 7-day leave passes and orders for each recruit's next assignment.

"You men are sailors now. Remember what that uniform stands for and all those who have worn it before you. I am proud of you and all you have accomplished here, and you should be, too.

You came as kids, but now you leave as men and a part of the greatest Navy in the world. Now, I need you to fall in so we can get this show started."

No one had time to look at their next assignment, tucking the papers into their footlockers for when they returned. They gathered outside, shaking hands and having a smoke, when they heard, "Okay, field strip those butts and fall in!"

As they waited for the ceremony to begin, Phillip looked toward the crowd gathering in the bleachers to see if Jim and

Anna might have made it. "Anchors Aweigh" started playing. That was their cue to march. They proceeded past the crowds to their seats. They listened to speeches from the base commander, the recruit trainers, and a couple of civilians they had never heard of.

Finally, it was time. The Master Chief stepped to the mic and said, "I present to you the Navy's newest sailors." The music started as they passed in review.

Once they got close to the podium, they heard the command, "Eyes right!" and each turned to look at the crowd. The officers by the podium stood and rendered a hand salute. Just as the Chief said, "Ready front," Phillip thought he caught a glimpse of his mom in the stands. But he had to be mistaken.

They were dismissed as family, and friends came onto the parade grounds.

From behind, he heard a familiar voice say, "Hey there, sailor."

Phillip turned, and there they were. Anna gave him a long hug while Jim waited to shake his hand.

"I didn't think you would make it," Phillip said.

"We figured since you got seven days' leave, you might enjoy a ride instead of taking the plane," Jim replied.

Phillip took them around and introduced them to his friends and DIs, hoping they wouldn't embarrass him too much with some of the stories they could tell.

It took about an hour to pack his duffel bags and head out to the car. As he heard that screen door slam for the last time, he smiled. He had made memories here he would share for a lifetime and had grown up more than he thought possible. He was glad to have this adventure behind him. Jim helped load his stuff in the car and said, "You ready to go home?"

"Yes, sir," Phillip replied.

Jim laughed and said, "Sir? Didn't you learn anything? I was a sergeant and had to work for my living when I was in the Army."

"I know, Dad, but 'sir' also shows respect. Let's go home."

Jim slapped Phillip on the back and said, "Yes, let's go home."

Chapter 12 : Between Two Worlds

On the drive home, Anna asked Phillip if he knew where he was going from there. Phillip said he had received his orders, but with everything that was going on, he hadn't had a chance to open them. He dug through his duffel bag, pulled out the envelope, and read it aloud.

"Airman McManus, you are to report for specialized training:

- Hospital Corps 'A' School (12 weeks)
- Location: San Antonio, Texas
- Date: October 6, 1969
- Purpose: Training on basic principles and techniques of patient care and first aid procedures.

Transportation: A Navy bus will be available for transport to the Naval base once you arrive by commercial air. Tickets enclosed.

Required items: Bring all military-issued clothing and equipment provided to you by the Navy.

Note: Enclosed are insignia showing your promotion to E3. Ensure all your uniforms display the correct rank upon arrival at the Naval base."

Anna noted she had some sewing to do. Phillip thanked her but insisted that he would get them sewn on while he was home. Jim, on the other hand, just snickered and said, "Texas! Lucky you," recalling his own days in Abilene, Texas, during the war.

As they entered town, Jim asked Phillip if he was hungry. Phillip was always hungry, so Jim said, "Where do you want to stop?"

"I think you know," Phillip said, and Jim nodded.

"Okay, Canteen it is."

After their meal, Phillip walked into the house, went back to his bedroom, and put his bag down. He looked around the room, making a mental note that everything was exactly the same as before he left. He quickly changed into some civilian clothes and came out to the living room.

"Are you going anywhere tonight?" Anna asked. Phillip said no, he wasn't. It had been a long day; he was tired, and all he wanted to do was just talk and get caught up on any news—something they didn't get at basic training. Not even the Stars and Stripes newspaper.

Jim told Phillip the Cubs had a major meltdown in September, blowing a seven-game lead over the Mets and missing the playoffs.

"So, who won the World Series?" Phillip asked.

"The Mets won the World Series, beating the Orioles in five games," Jim explained. "Oh, and there was a big music gathering in a place in New York called Woodstock where a lot of hippies went to smoke pot and listen to loud music. But other than that, nothing new to report."

Phillip leaned back in his chair, taking in the familiar surroundings of home. It felt strange to be back, even if just for a short while before heading to Texas. The thought about his new assignment—medical training—made him wonder how difficult it was going to be. Maybe he should have paid more attention in anatomy class his senior year.

"Hospital Corps," Anna said. "That's good, isn't it? You'll be helping people."

Phillip nodded. "Yeah, I guess so. Better than some alternatives."

Jim caught Phillip's eye, silently signaling that he

probably shouldn't tell his mom that Navy Corpsmen were assigned to Marines since they were part of the Navy. If Phillip didn't know where he was going yet, there was no need to add to her worries about the boys.

"How long will you be home before you have to leave?" Anna asked, already mentally planning the meals she'd cook for him.

"Just a week," Phillip replied. "Enough time to get some real food in me and maybe catch up with a few friends if they're around."

Phillip was up as the sun came through the window. Anna apologized if she was making too much noise.

"No, it isn't the noise that woke me up," he said. "It was the light."

"You want something to eat?" Anna asked, already bustling around the kitchen with the familiar rhythm that had comforted him throughout childhood.

"No, I think I'll go downtown to the Coffee Cup and stop by Brown's to say hello. Do you have any idea where the keys to my car are?" His voice carried a hint of excitement at having the simple pleasure of just driving a car again.

"Hanging on the wall next to the coat rack," she replied without looking up from the dishes she was washing.

Phillip asked Anna if she needed anything while he was out, noticing how she seemed both older and exactly the same as before he'd left.

She had a little grayer hair than he remembered and hoped it wasn't from worrying about him or his brothers.

"No, I'm good," she said, her hands still immersed in soapy water. Then added, "Will you be home for dinner tonight?"

"Yes," Phillip said, suddenly aware of how few family dinners remained before Texas. "What are we having?"

"Your dad wants liver and onions. Is that okay with you?"

"Sounds fine," he said as he kissed Anna on the cheek and headed out the door.

Since he didn't have much hair, he had put on his Navy stocking cap and a light coat that felt too thin against the morning chill. As he drove through the familiar streets, he reminisced about his younger days exploring every corner of town from the seat of his StingRay bike. It had been a while since Phillip had driven, so as he settled behind the wheel, he tuned the radio to KIOA, the station that played mostly rock. A Peter, Paul, and Mary song began playing, and Phillip found himself singing along to "Leaving on a Jet Plane," knowing all too well that was exactly what he would soon be doing.

Phillip stopped in at Brown's and saw Helen and Don. Their faces lit up with recognition. They asked about basic training and how long he was going to be home.

"It looks like you have put on a few pounds," Don said.

Phillip laughed. "I don't know how that was possible with all the pushups they had me do."

It had only been six weeks, but it wasn't the same. The town seemed smaller somehow, quieter, too. Most of his former classmates were gone, either at college or work, chasing their own futures. Phillip drove by the high school, memories of crowded hallways and Friday night games flooding back. He stopped in at the mission to shoot a couple of games of nine-ball. After the third game, he decided it was time to head home.

Before going home, he decided to stop at Shaul Cemetery. Standing before the simple headstone of his grandfather's grave, he felt like no time had passed at all. He told him about basic training, where he was heading off to next, and how much he missed their chats while sitting on the porch swing, watching the summer storms roll in.

"You'd be proud of your grandsons, Grandpa," he whispered, his voice catching slightly. Before Phillip left, he brushed off Grandpa Craig's headstone and straightened the little American flag the Legion had put on his grave.

Climbing back into the car, he passed through Wildwood Park, where he'd spent countless summer days as a kid and a place he used to sit if he just needed some time to himself. As he headed home, the familiar streets both comforting and strange, he felt caught between two worlds. "Maybe I'll call Max and see if he and Rodney have any plans later in the evening," he thought, eager to reconnect with the friends who still understood who he used to be and have one more evening before he became who he was becoming. Everything was changing, and so was he.

After supper, a car drove into the driveway. It was Max and Rodney. The boys came in, saying hi to Jim and Anna asking if Phillip was home. Phillip was coming out of the bathroom when he saw their familiar faces.

"Hey there, what happened to your hair?" Rodney joked.

Phillip ran his hand over his head, saying, "It's growing back."

The boys sat, talked, and reminisced about the past, asking a lot of questions about basic training and where and when he was going next, which Phillip tried to answer. Max had gotten a job at John Morrell's meat packing plant, and Rodney was working in the parts department at Vaughn's Chevrolet. Phillip inquired about a few other kids that came to his mind, like Fisher, the pool shark who was in the Army; Anne, who was at Drake and was probably the prettiest girl in their class. And Kay, a girl who had a smile that could light up a room, who was also in college, but they didn't know where.

They talked and laughed until ten, and when the news came on KTVO, the local station, both of them realized they had better call it a night because they had to work tomorrow. They said goodbye and made plans for the weekend to shoot some pool and get something to eat.

Phillip sat down with his dad, acknowledging that there was a lot of change in what was on the news. Tonight's story was covering the Vietnam Moratorium Day event, where millions of Americans participated in protests against the war. Anna, watching the events unfold, said, "I think these demonstrations aren't helping because, besides the significant disruption in daily life, they're increasing the political tension considerably. Can't they trust that our government knows what they're doing?"

Phillip just said, "I think they lost that trust in 1963."

The days passed by quickly, and with his departure date drawing near, Phillip felt a mix of excitement and apprehension as he focused on getting ready. He had his recently earned rank sewn on—a small symbol of his achievements that filled him with some pride. He worked on packing everything he needed into his navy duffel bag, the familiar smells bringing back memories of basic training. He also pulled down the suitcase Don had given him as a graduation present. Phillip packed a few civilian clothes that, this time, he could take with him.

Anna appeared in the doorway, hesitating for a moment, watching her son—no longer her little boy but a young man. She asked softly if he needed any help.

Phillip looked up and smiled at his mother, recognizing the familiar gesture. "I'm good, Mom, thanks," he replied, carefully folding a shirt the way he'd been taught. After a moment's pause, he asked if Anna had planned anything for dinner, changing the subject.

"Well, we're going to the grocery store when your dad gets off work, so I figured loose meat hamburgers."

Phillip's face lit up, and he laughed with genuine pleasure. "One of my favorite meals!"

Something he knew he'd miss when he went back to the Navy. "That sounds good, but if it is okay tonight, I thought, if you'll let me, I would treat you and Dad to supper at Mollie's." A place the family used to go for celebrations throughout his childhood.

Anna protested, saying, "Oh, you don't need to do that. You should save your money—you might need it when you get to Texas."

Phillip stood and crossed the room, placing his hands reassuringly on her shoulders. "I have plenty," he insisted with the confidence of someone newly independent, "because I didn't have much need to spend when I was at basic, and they'll give me more. I think I am good.

Besides, the Navy pretty much takes care of our basic needs."

Anna, understanding that he wanted to demonstrate his independence as well as growing into an adult, said, "Well, that would be nice," as she patted his hand. "Let me talk to your dad when he gets home."

D-Day came too soon as they headed out the door to Des Moines. Jim looked over his shoulder and asked Phillip if he wanted to stop at the canteen. Phillip said no, insisting he had had plenty while he was home.

"How about we stop in Pella at Jaarsma Bakery to get some Dutch letters and maybe a pecan roll for the flight?"

Anna agreed. "I have a few favorite items I, too, would like to get."

As they finished the drive, Jim asked Phillip if he knew where he would be going after his training. Phillip said he didn't know but said, according to Art, they give you a wish where you can write down three requests. Anna asked if he had anything in mind. Phillip thought for a minute and said, "Well, I am a sailor, so I would think a sea assignment would be good. I can't imagine how small one must feel when you're out there in the middle of nowhere on a ship."

As they waited for the call to board, Anna asked, "Do you think you will be home in time for Christmas?" Phillip didn't answer right away but finally said, "I don't think so."

At the airport, Jim and Anna once again said goodbye. As Anna was hugging her son, she started to tear up because this time, she didn't know when she would see him again.

Phillip hugged his mom and said, "Don't worry about me, Mom. I am going to be fine. I will write and call when I can. You just focus on taking care of you and Dad and understand the Navy will take care of me." Phillip didn't look back this time because he did not want his last thought of home to be seeing his mother cry.

Behind him, Jim's arm encircled Anna's shoulders as they watched their son—now a small figure in uniform—disappear, carrying their hearts with him into an uncertain but promising future.

Chapter 13: Corpsman

The flight from Des Moines to San Antonio would take about four hours. Phillip made himself as comfortable as you can on a plane. When the flight attendant came by, he asked if he could have a cup of coffee. She said of course and asked if he needed cream and sugar. Nodding yes, as he awaited the coffee to arrive, he took out one of the Dutch letters.

The passenger sitting next to him looked at it and said, "May I ask what that is?"

Phillip smiled and said, "It is a Dutch letter." The passenger seemed confused. Phillip added, "It is a little bit of heaven wrapped up in a pastry." Tearing it in half, he handed it to her.

Phillip's coffee arrived, and he and Sue, a young lady about his age, sat and talked for the next four hours. She was from Minneapolis, Minnesota, on her way back to San Antonio to start her junior year at Texas A&M, where she was majoring in Education. They kept each other company until the wheels touched down in San Antonio. Sue gave

Phillip a hug, said goodbye, and thanked him for the "little piece of heaven" he had shared earlier and especially for keeping her mind off flying, which she hated.

"Good luck at school," Phillip said as he turned and walked towards baggage claim.

Upon arrival at the Navy base, Phillip went through the administration route where he was assigned his barracks, got additional uniforms for corpsmen, and a schedule for the next 24 hours. After touring the base to see what was available, he made his way over to his new home.

Unlike basic training, his new facilities were set up like a dorm. Four bedrooms with two bunks, two tables and chairs, a larger wall locker, and, of course, the footlocker at the end of his rack. There was also a common room that the eight sailors would share containing two couches, a table with chairs, and a coffee pot for when they were burning the midnight oil studying.

Phillip stored his gear, made his bed, and walked out to meet his new shipmates. There were only six, counting himself, currently there, each sitting in the common room getting acquainted. The first sailor said hello to Phillip and introduced himself. He was John Thornton, from Houston. He stood about 6 feet with dark hair and broad shoulders.

The second sailor was from California. His name was Carlos Martinez, a Hispanic who was just a little over 5 feet with jet-black hair. From New Jersey was Sam Adams, who was the same height as Phillip, 5' 9" with red hair and a scar above his right eye. Then there was John Brown from Montana, a true cowboy standing 6' 3" who walked like he spent a lot of time on a horse, and finally Phillip met Brent Williams who hailed from Ohio. Brent was just short of 6 feet with blond hair and a tattoo of a buckeye on his left bicep. Phillip said hello and introduced himself.

They all laughed as each shared a special story about themselves. Phillip felt himself relaxing; the tension he'd been carrying since stepping foot on base began to dissolve. These were just guys like him, thrown together by the Navy and making the best of it.

Thornton stood up and walked to the mini-fridge in the corner. "Anyone want a soda?" He tossed a can to Phillip without waiting for an answer.

"So Phillip, why did you choose Hospital Corpsman?" he asked. Phillip caught the soda one-handed and popped it open. It was the first personal question anyone had asked him since enlisting. Now, facing these five men who would be his roommates and classmates for the foreseeable future, he considered how much to share.

"I guess of the choices they offered, it seemed to be the safest and maybe offer me an opportunity when I get out," Phillip responded.

The room grew quiet for a minute after Lopez told them that corpsmen don't seem to have a very good life span if they end up with the Marines in Vietnam. Phillip glanced around the room, taking in the faces of these men who would share his journey through corpsman training.

A schedule pinned to the bulletin board caught his eye: 0500 wake-up call, PT at 0530, breakfast at 0645, classes beginning at 0800. The beginning of a very rigorous and demanding training. A training that had a 25% washout rating.

The conversation flowed easily as the night wore on. The last two guys arrived just as the base PA system announced lights out. Phillip would have to get to know them tomorrow.

As he climbed into his rack, listening to the unfamiliar sounds settling around him, Phillip thought about the journey ahead. Corpsman school would be challenging—he'd heard stories of the intense medical training, the pressure to perform under stress, and the endless terminology to memorize, something he wasn't particularly good at. But looking across at Brown, already asleep and thinking of the others in the rooms nearby, Phillip felt a sense of camaraderie forming.

0500 arrived soon enough, and Phillip got a chance to meet the last two men from last night over breakfast. John Ferguson was from New York, a stocky guy with a buzz cut who spoke with a rapid-fire cadence. Robert Ness was from Minnesota, tall and fair, with a very noticeable Swedish accent.

After chow, they walked over to the classroom, where they were met by several Navy Corpsmen in crisp uniforms. In the front of the room was Chief Petty Officer Vaughan, a man with salt-and-pepper hair cropped close to his scalp. You could tell he was experienced and had seen combat up close. He had the kind of steady gaze that could evaluate everyone in seconds. He welcomed them and laid out the objective for the next 12 weeks.

"So, I hope you like the accommodations of the Liberty Barracks," Chief Vaughan began. "It was designed to give you the best chance to succeed here. The coffee pot in your common room? Use it. The extra desk space? Use it. The quiet hours? Respect them. Because what you're about to undertake isn't high school."

He continued, "The purpose of Navy Corpsman Training is to provide advanced training and expertise to hospital corpsmen in the Navy, focusing on specialized skills and roles beyond basic first aid. This training is crucial for preparing corpsmen to serve in various roles, including field surgical techniques, suturing, IV administration of drugs, and stabilizing patients for transport from the field to the base hospital. Do you have any questions at this point?"

"No, Chief," came the response.

The Chief continued, "You will learn hands-on techniques, including Basic Life Support, medical terminology, anatomy, and physiology. The training methods include course lectures, demonstrations, online materials, simulations, and laboratory practice. You will have to perform exercises, written exams, and clinical practicums that will be evaluated to determine your knowledge and skills for passing this training. There are 50 of you starting this training. But history tells us that 25% of you will wash out at some point during this training."

The room was dead silent. They had heard rumors of this, but now the Chief had just confirmed that it was true.

"Take a good look around and decide if you are going to be one of the 13 who won't be here at the end. Or will you be amongst the best to call yourself corpsman?" The chief's eyes swept across the room, seeming to make a quick evaluation of each student. "Navy Medicine's motto is 'Corpsmen save lives.' It isn't just a slogan—it's your purpose. When a Marine is bleeding out on the battlefield, when a sailor is having a heart attack in the middle of the ocean when a child is brought to your aid station, you are the difference between life and death."

The chief nodded to one of the petty officers, who began distributing thick textbooks to each student.

"Now, open up your Anatomy books, and let's get started looking at the human skeleton."

As Phillip opened his textbook, he caught Lopez's eye across the aisle, who gave him a small nod as if to say, "We've got this." Phillip nodded back, then turned his attention to the diagrams of the human skeleton on the page before him. Twelve weeks suddenly seemed both too long and not nearly enough time.

The lecture proceeded at a blistering pace. By the time they broke for lunch, Phillip's hand was cramped from taking notes, and his brain felt like it was swimming in medical

156

terminology.

"Jesus," Sam muttered as they filed out of the classroom. "I think I've learned more in four hours than I did in my entire senior year of high school."

"This is just day one," Thornton reminded them. "We've got 83 more to go."

As they headed to the mess hall, Phillip, along with his new friends, recalled what the chief had said: corpsmen save lives. And that's exactly what Phillip was determined to learn how to do.

After lunch, they headed to the hospital. The rest of the day would be an extensive tour of each ward. The burn unit seemed to have a negative effect on Williams, the kid from Ohio, who had to excuse himself as he ran to the head to throw up.

The Chief watched Williams exit and said to the class, "You're not going to help anyone by throwing up. You have to focus on the injury, not the person. Do you understand me?"

"Yes, Chief," came the response. They went through the ER, the surgical wing, looked in at the critical care and coronary care units, and stopped in at the pediatrics and birthing areas last before being dismissed for the day. Their homework was to learn the bones of the arms and legs and to be ready to pass an exam in the morning.

The week flew by, and as originally stated, by week 4, the 50 sailors who started were down to 45. The only person going from their dorm was Williams, the kid from Ohio. It wasn't that he couldn't handle the academic requirements; he couldn't handle the sight of blood. Chief Vaughan had pulled Williams aside after his third episode in the trauma simulation lab, and by the next morning, his bunk was empty, and his belongings were gone.

"Down to 7," Thornton had said grimly at breakfast that day. "Wonder who's next?"

Phillip had experienced a couple of close calls himself, scoring just above the standard set for passing, but he was still there. The skeletal system exam had nearly done him in—he'd mixed up the carpals and tarsals—but he'd managed to scrape by with a 72, two points above failing. Memorizing was difficult for Phillip, as he was more of a hands-on learner.

But with help from his dorm mates, especially Martinez, who seemed to have a photographic memory, he was moving into practical application.

The daily routine was grueling: 0500 PT, breakfast, four hours of classroom instruction, lunch, and then four more hours of practical application in the hospital. By evening chow, most of them were mentally exhausted but still faced several hours of studying before taps.

Phillip spent most of his off time writing letters, doing laundry, or studying, as there was no way he was washing out.

On one Saturday night, he, along with Thornton, Adams, Ness, and his roommate and best friend Martinez, went to the post theater to watch "Woodstock." After the show and a few well-deserved beers at the EM club, they could be seen—and heard—walking back to their dorm singing the song from Country Joe and the Fish: "And it's one, two, three, what are we fighting for? Don't ask me, I don't give a damn, next stop is Vietnam."

It was a good thing the next day was Sunday, where there was no PT or training because sleep, praying to the porcelain god, and coffee occupied most of the day.

They practiced on each other, giving shots, remembering to pull back the syringe to make sure they weren't in a vein, and starting IVs.

Their arms looked like they had lost a fight with the Tasmanian Devil from the black and blue marks as they blew through veins.

"Try again," Phillip said to Ness, trying not to wince as Ness prepared for another attempt. "Remember, slide the needle beside the vein, then angle it over slowly until you see blood coming into the tube."

Phillip watched Ness's face scrunched in concentration. The Swedish sailor's hands were steady, but Phillip could tell he was nervous about missing again.

After the third poke, Ness's eyes lit up. "I got it!" he exclaimed, relief washing over his face.

Phillip put the third bandage on his arm, saying, "See? Piece of cake." He'd need to wear long sleeves to hide the evidence of their practice session. That was all part of the training—learning to endure the discomfort to master a skill needed in the field.

Chapter 14: Heart, Mind, and Strength: The Corpsman's Journey

The last sailor out of the liberty barracks was Brent Williams from New York. At twenty-eight, Williams was the oldest of the group. Despite his age, or perhaps because of it, Williams never developed the hunger for medical knowledge that drove the others. He consistently traded study time for hours at the Enlisted Men's club, nursing beers and swapping stories with sailors from other units. The remaining men watched silently as he packed his seabag, folding each uniform item with the precise efficiency of someone who'd moved around his whole life.

"What's next?" Adams asked, his voice betrayed a hint of envy, not for Williams washing out, but for the unknown possibilities that awaited beyond their rigorous training.

"Not sure," Williams replied with a half-smile that never reached his eyes. "But probably headed to some ship somewhere in the Pacific."

The shrug that accompanied his words suggested both uncertainty and a practiced indifference that had become his shield. He hefted his seabag over his shoulder with a grunt, the canvas bulging with his possessions, and offered a casual salute that somehow managed to be both respectful and dismissive.

As the door swung shut, the Cowboy, in a thick drawl, said, "One more casualty."

He made a small tally mark in the notebook he always carried. Their barracks were down to six men now, six who had survived the intellectual and physical gauntlet that Hospital Corpsman training had become.

Some things didn't change. Dressing at 0500 hours and outside for PT at 0530. Depending on the weather, they would run for two or three miles. Then, they would come back to barracks for a quick shower, shave, and get dressed before heading over to the dining facility for breakfast. On the way back, hearing the notes, stopping midstride, raising a hand in salute as the National Anthem officially started their day. Then to class.

They were spending less time in the classroom now and getting more hands-on experience. They worked with both the doctors and the nurses, polishing their skills. Each morning, there was a list that indicated which ward they would be in. Phillip liked the surgical suite first, then the Emergency room and finally the birthing ward. Phillip wrote home telling Anna that there wasn't anything more amazing than seeing and being able to help bring a new soul into the world.

During their training, they learned that chicken skin could be used to practice suturing. It was a common and cost-effective method for medical students and surgeons to hone their skills. The texture and feel of chicken skin were similar enough to human skin to provide a realistic practice environment, allowing trainees to develop proficiency in various suturing techniques. Phillip spent extra hours practicing, determined to master every stitch, and making sure each stitch was perfect and closing the wound without overlapping the skin.

His dedication paid off during his surgical rotation. While assisting in an abdominal procedure, Phillip maintained steady hands as the surgeon cut into the patient. Phillip used a sterile lap pad to wipe away the blood, find the bleeders and clamp them off using small mosquito clamps. He watched the surgeon close the peritoneum, a tissue that lines the abdominal wall and covers most of the organs in the abdomen. After finishing this critical layer, the doctor turned to Phillip.

"You finish up," he said, handing over the instruments. "Use a 1/2-inch circle reverse needle with 5.0 nylon." Then, he walked out.

Phillip was beaming with pride to be trusted by the surgeon to finish. His hands didn't waver as he placed each suture with precision, recalling all the hours of practice. The next day, he discovered the surgeon had sent a note to Phillip's Chief highlighting his skills and steady hands, suggesting Phillip should get more specialized training in surgery because of his natural aptitude. As he read the note, Phillip felt a surge of purpose. Perhaps this was the path he was meant to follow.

As he sat on the couch, having a smoke, Phillip read the letter he got from his mom and dad.

Anna had written that her brother, Uncle Art, had died. It was sudden and a surprise, considering he was only 46. She said that there was no reason to interrupt his training for him to come home for the funeral, and because he wasn't immediate family, even contacting the Red Cross wouldn't help secure emergency leave. Phillip thought of the sadness his mom must feel losing her little brother and now having only her mother, Mary, left.

Phillip folded the letter carefully and placed it back in its envelope. He stared at the ceiling, wondering if he should write back tonight or wait until morning when his thoughts might be clearer. The grief felt distant here, surrounded by uniforms and routine, but he knew it would hit him when he finally got home. For now, he had to focus on completing his training. That's what Uncle Art would have wanted.

The men were sitting around the barracks, having some sodas and reading through medical reports. That evening's homework was to look at photos of injuries, read the explanation of what happened, and then write out what treatment they would follow to stabilize the patient for transportation to a hospital. No detail could be left out. This was a group effort, so they would be expected to brief the rest of their class, explaining their assessment and defending their treatment choices.

After their presentation, they would get feedback from the class, other Corpsmen who have had experience with these injuries, and the chief. Often, gunshot wounds were the most complicated to assess, based on whether the round exited the body or bounced around inside. This was all a part of the final exam that would be taken in week 12.

Ness tossed a photo on the table and said, "I'm telling you, this lac with the embedded debris is going to be a nightmare to present."

Thornton rubbed his eyes. "Do you want the penetrating chest wound with a pneumothorax? If we miss a single step on the tension assessment, we're toast."

The barracks had fallen quiet, punctuated only by the occasional tapping of a pencil. They were in week 10, and the pressure was mounting. They had already mastered basic trauma care, but these complex case studies pushed them to think critically under pressure, just as they would need to do in the field.

Phillip nodded; their training demanded precision— decisions made in seconds that could save lives. Tomorrow's presentation would test not just their medical knowledge but their ability to defend decisions under the scrutiny of experienced field medics who had treated similar wounds in actual combat situations.

They agreed on the penetrating chest wound with a pneumothorax. They would present as a group and defend it together. They felt confident they had it right, as they closed their books and turned in for the night.

The final weeks were spent at the hospital. Phillip often volunteered for extra duty, believing that he could learn more there than by having his head buried in a textbook—he could do that in the evening when he was back at the barracks. He spent hours in the ER watching, learning, and developing skills he would use later.

One day, a sailor was brought in with a knife wound, an accident in the kitchen. The knife had cut into the femoral artery. With every beat of the heart, blood was pumping out of the wound. Phillip was instructed to hop on the gurney and apply pressure as the patient was taken to surgery. Once in the surgical suite, the surgeon told Phillip to hop down; they had it from there. As Phillip walked back toward the ER, he noticed the stares, not so much at him but at the amount of blood that was soaking through his uniform.

"Jesus, McManus," said Lieutenant Moss, the ER nurse, when she saw him. "You look like you walked off the set of a horror movie."

Phillip glanced down at himself. The blood had soaked through his uniform from chest to knees. Some had splashed onto his forearms and hands, and he could feel it drying in the creases of his skin.

The Lieutenant winced. "Is he going to make it?"

"Think so. They got him into surgery pretty quick. I had to ride the gurney to keep pressure on it."

"Well, go get cleaned up," she said, handing him a fresh set of scrubs from the supply cabinet.

In the shower, Phillip watched the water run red, then pink, then clear. He scrubbed his hands and arms, paying special attention to his fingernails.

When he emerged from the locker room in fresh scrubs, his hair still damp, the ER was busier than when he had left it. A car accident had brought in three patients

"McManus," the lieutenant said, "that was good work. OR just called down—they've stabilized him. Looks like he'll pull through."

"Thank you, ma'am," Phillip said, feeling a weight lift from his chest that he hadn't realized was there.

"First time dealing with an arterial bleed?"

"Yes, ma'am."

"How are you feeling?"

Phillip considered the question. "Honestly? A little shaky."

"Get something to eat, have some juice. We have everything here, we got this," Lieutenant Moss told him.

Later that night, as he finally headed back to the barracks, Phillip thought about the cook. The man would have a long recovery ahead, and Phillip had played a part in making that possible.

The realization settled into him. This was his calling: to be a healer. To make a difference when it mattered most.

Week 12 had arrived, which meant everyone was preparing for their final exam. It would cover a wide range of medical knowledge and skills, including topics like medical terminology, anatomy and physiology, basic life support, emergency medical technician protocols, as well as various patient care aspects.

Everyone had passed the practical part, so now they just had to focus on the written portion of the exam. The tests were handed out, and they were told they had two hours to complete them. Once done, they could bring their work up to the desk and be dismissed for the day. Results would be posted the next morning in the classroom.

Phillip looked at the clock and then over to Martinez, who had already started. He read each question carefully as well as each answer, not wanting to make the same mistake he did last time. He worked methodically through each page. If he wasn't sure of an answer, he would skip it for now, hoping another question might help him when he revisited it.

He got to the bones in the wrist and was thankful that Ness had given him a trick to ensure he got it right: "Some Lovers Try Positions That They Can't Handle," which represents the bones in order: Scaphoid, Lunate, Triquetrum, Pisiform, Trapezium, Trapezoid, Capitate, and Hamate.

Finally, Phillip reached the end. He went back to questions he'd skipped. He was done, in more ways than one. He turned in his test and materials, noticing on his way out that most had already finished and there were still thirty minutes on the clock.

Phillip walked over to the barracks to find everyone there.

"Well, how did you do?" asked Cowboy.

"Good. I had to guess a few, but since the Navy likes B, I went with that."

Adams laughed and said he did the same. Ness looked at the clock and said, "We have a couple of hours before chow. What do you all say we change into some real clothes and go get a couple of beers?"

It was a long, sleepless night as they stayed up and talked. Thornton said, "I heard no one fails. You may have to repeat a certain course, but we did it."

Phillip was confident that the high score he got in his practicals would help in any area where he might have faltered.

The next morning, after breakfast, the group walked to the classroom. They stood in the back, waiting for their turn to see the post.

Thornton was first up and noticed the results were simply posted as either "go" or "no go," and he didn't see any names on the "no go" side. The Navy wasn't concerned about who was top of the class or who got what score. You either passed or you didn't.

He yelled back to the others, "Come look! We are officially Corpsmen now!"

Pats on the backs and sighs of relief could be heard as the results became known. Thorton said, "We started with 50 and now we are 39, beat the odds."

Below was this simple motto reminding them of who they were now:

"I WILL DEDICATE MY HEART, MIND, AND STRENGTH TO THE WORK BEFORE ME."

And next to it was the caduceus—the symbol worn by Corpsmen with two snakes intertwining a staff capped by two wings.

Chapter 15: Home for the Holidays

It was December 18, 1969, two days before graduation. The days were busy getting ready for the ceremonies, marching, writing home, even if you would beat the letter. And getting their personal belongings squared away so when it was time to go, they could go.

Phillip received a letter from home letting him know that both Art and Raymond would be home. It seems Raymond got an early out and was going to be a civilian again. And Art was home from air traffic control school, waiting orders. Anna wrote, "I know you said you probably won't make it, but know we are so proud of you and hope you can get home soon." Phillip laid down the letter and snickered, saying to himself, 'Sooner than you think.'

Graduation day came, and along with their certificates of training came orders promoting them, and some had orders of where they would go next. Phillip, being a reserve, would be going home, waiting for orders for his next assignment, which would arrive later.

Phillip carefully stitched his 3rd class petty officer stripes onto his uniform—a single red stripe on blue. Above the stripe was the Caduceus, and an eagle above that. His fingers moved with the same precision he'd learned to apply to sutures. This was sewing Phillip didn't mind doing. Each stitch represented twelve weeks of sweat, study, and sacrifice. When he was done, he looked at it, running his thumb over the Caduceus—he was no longer just a recruit; he was now Hospital Corpsman Third Class.

The barracks had a buzz as everyone packed their seabags. Men who'd been strangers three months ago now shared a bond that civilians could never understand. They'd seen each other at their worst—exhausted, frustrated, sometimes even ready to drop out—and at their best, rising to challenges none of them thought possible.

After saying goodbye to everyone, Phillip stood face-to-face with Martinez. The lump in his throat surprised him.

"I hope our paths cross again," Phillip said, his voice steadier than he felt. "But if they don't, I'm glad they came together here."

He gripped Martinez's shoulder. "I don't know if I would have made it through those first weeks if it wasn't for you."

Martinez laughed, the sound echoing in the nearly empty room. "Oh, I don't know how you stood there letting me stick you over and over again until I finally got it right. And then say, 'Do it again.' I think we're even." His smile faded to something more serious. "Save lives out there, McManus."

"You too, Martinez."

They shook hands—a firm grip that said everything words couldn't—as Phillip hoisted his seabag and caught a ride to the airport.

The Navy provided a ticket, but it was for standby, and Phillip was hoping he would be able to get on a plane. The navy cared about you getting to your assignment, but home was another issue. The airport terminal hummed with chaotic energy, packed with travelers in various states of holiday panic. But why not? In five days, it would be Christmas, and it looked like everyone was going somewhere.

Phillip's mother didn't know he was coming home. His last letter had deliberately been vague—"hoping to be home sometime after the New Year." The thought of surprising her made the inconvenience of standby worth it. After all those nights she'd spent worrying about him, he wanted to give her this one perfect moment.

He was told to go to Gate 5 and present his ticket to the agent. If any seats were available after boarding, he could also board. The plane was departing at 1530 hours. And if he didn't catch that flight, there would be one more departing at 2200 hours.

Phillip found a seat with a view of the runway. He lit a cigarette, the familiar ritual calming his nerves as he enjoyed a cup of coffee. Around him, civilians rushed in all directions, their urgency a stark contrast to the military's "hurry up and wait" mentality he'd internalized over the past three months.

Boarding began, and Phillip watched as each passenger slowly made their way to the plane—a businessman with a briefcase, a young mother trying to manage two small children. The more that went, the more doubtful he grew that he would get on. His eyes drifted to the USO sign visible down the concourse. Once the last passenger walked down the ramp. The ticket agent—her name tag read Gloria—called him to come up front.

"Sorry, sailor, but the flight's full," she said, genuine regret in her eyes.

"That's okay. I'll try again tonight," Phillip replied, his disappointment hidden behind the composure his training had instilled in him. Phillip asked the agent if he could leave his bag there and go down to the USO club.

"I can keep an eye on them," the agent replied.

Phillip took off his pea coat and made the short walk to the USO. The United Service Organizations was a private, nonprofit organization that provided support to U.S. military personnel and their families.

Phillip walked in and saw service members from all branches doing what he was trying to do—get home. He grabbed a sandwich and a coffee and sat down to wait. Some were sleeping, some were playing cards, but most were just waiting.

At 2100 hours, Phillip returned to the gate. Seeing the size of the crowd already there made it hard to think this flight was going to be any different. The plane started to board as Phillip thought about spending the night back down at the USO club.

The agent once again signaled for Phillip to come over. She asked, "Is your family expecting you tonight?"

Phillip nodded sideways, telling her that he was hoping to surprise them, so if he didn't make it home, they wouldn't be disappointed.

With that, the agent said, "Follow me." She led him out to the plane, where a baggage agent took his bags, and onto the plane they went.

Phillip looked around and couldn't see an empty seat. He looked confused when the flight attendant said, "You can sit here."

First class? Phillip was shocked as he climbed in and fastened his seat belt.

The plane was airborne for the four-hour flight home. He enjoyed the large seat, the extra legroom, and the beer she gave him without carding or charging him for it. As he looked out upon the darkness, he reminded himself of the need to catch some shut-eye. Tomorrow was going to be a long day.

They landed in Des Moines around 0225. By the time he had collected his bags and stepped outside, it was after 0300. Snowflakes drifted lazily from the dark sky, dancing in the glow of the streetlights. Phillip felt the gentle sting of cold against his cheeks.

'Looks like we'll have a white Christmas after all,' he thought to himself.

The streets were empty as he hailed a cab, the only moving vehicle in sight, and asked if the driver could take him to the Greyhound station.

They arrived at the station, and as Phillip pulled out his wallet, the cabbie said, "Welcome back, son. This one's on me." It reminded him of the kind of people who live in Iowa. Respectful, kind, and hardworking.

Phillip bought a ticket to Ottumwa, set to leave around 0500. He settled into one of the hard plastic chairs in the waiting area, surrounded by a handful of other travelers. He felt exhaustion, but even that couldn't dampen his spirits, knowing every mile got him closer to home.

He arrived in Ottumwa as morning broke across the horizon, washing the sky in pale shades of pink and gold. Phillip walked over to Hoffman's Drug, where he caught a city bus to complete his journey. The bus let him off a few blocks from home, and he hoisted his duffel bag onto his shoulder for the final stretch.

It was bitterly cold now, the temperature having dropped, and even his Navy pea coat couldn't keep the chill away from him. His breath formed clouds in front of him as he walked through the fresh snow.

As he rounded the corner onto his street, Phillip paused, taking in the sight of his family's home, spotting the

Christmas wreath hanging on the front door. He checked the mailbox and found his letter still waiting to be delivered. Thinking it had arrived quicker than he thought, but was glad no one picked it up yesterday.

"I guess I can deliver this myself," he murmured, tucking the envelope into his pocket.

It was 0915 on a Sunday morning. As he approached the house, Phillip peered through the kitchen window and saw his mother, Anna, working on the breakfast dishes. He looked at the familiar movements—the way she stacked plates after she dried each one.

"Well, it's now or never," he whispered to himself as he quietly turned the doorknob and stepped inside, the warmth of the house.

Anna turned at the sound of the door and froze, a plate slipping from her fingers and shattering on the floor. For a moment, neither of them moved—a tableau of shock and joy suspended in time. In the next moment, she was running toward him, tears already streaming down her face.

From another room, his father's voice called out, "What's going on?"

"Jim! Come quick! Phillip's home!" Anna cried, her voice

breaking as she threw her arms around her son, pressing her face against his chest as if to convince herself he was real.

Loud footsteps echoed down the hall as Raymond and Art made it to the living room. Art, never one to miss an opportunity for humor, grinned broadly and clapped Phillip on the shoulder.

"What took so long? Did you have to recycle?"

Jim appeared, momentarily speechless at the sight of his son.

"Welcome home, son," Jim said as he reached for Phillip's bags. "Let me put these in your room."

The family moved to the living room, coffee in hand. Phillip settled into his old spot on the couch as the questions came rapid-fire, and Phillip answered them one by one, sharing stories of his trip, the first-class flight, and the cab driver.

Anna, sitting close to Phillip, asked, "Why didn't you call or write that you were coming home?"

With a smile, Phillip pulled the letter from his pocket and held it up. "I did," he said, the envelope now creased from its journey. "Do you want me to read it to you?"

Jim laughed, a deep, genuine sound that filled the room. "Reminds me of when I surprised your mother on leave back in WWII," he said, exchanging a knowing look with Anna. "She was hanging out laundry, if I remember correctly."

Anna looked around the room at her family with contentment etched on her face. Finally, her family was home together for Christmas. Her eyes glistened with tears, but her smile was happy.

"I don't need anything under the tree this year. I have the best gift a mother could ask for. I have my boys home for Christmas," she had said, sniffling.

Phillip felt a profound sense of peace in this moment. He was surrounded by the people who helped shape him, he was simply home—and there was no better place to be.

Christmas morning came, and after coffee, the family gathered around the tree to exchange gifts. Art was looking at the tree when he asked Anna if she missed the way they used to put the tinsel on the tree.

"You mean throwing it?" Anna replied. "I would have to spend hours pulling it off and placing it properly on the tree. So no, I don't miss that part."

Art chuckled. "The kids made such a mess of it. Remember how Raymond would just grab handfuls and toss them at the highest branches?"

"And most of it would end up on the floor," Anna said, shaking her head with a smile. "I'm perfectly happy with our simple ornaments these days."

After all the gifts were opened, Anna went into the kitchen to start breakfast. Raymond started reminiscing about earlier Christmases when they were children.

"Remember how we'd wake up around 2:30 in the morning?" Raymond said, grinning at his siblings. "We'd sneak out to the living room with a flashlight, only to be scolded by Dad and sent back to bed."

"And we'd repeat the same thing every thirty minutes, until they finally gave up and got out of bed."

Jim laughed. "You kids were relentless. I think one year we were up at 4 AM because you wouldn't stop coming back. Hell, half the time I had just gotten to bed from putting the toys together that you wanted Santa to bring."

Art and Phillip spent a lot of time visiting with former classmates over pizza or a game of pool, catching up with what was going on in their lives. They listened to them talk about first semesters at college, exams, and newfound freedom, all the while mentally comparing these experiences to what they had gone through in the Navy. The late-night study sessions that their friends complained about paled in comparison to the physical and mental challenges they had experienced. Campus meal plans seemed luxurious after months of mess hall food. These were the same kids as before, but both Art and Phillip knew they were on different paths now.

Phillip and Art had made arrangements with their parents to host a New Year's Eve party. Jim asked if there was going to be alcohol involved.

"If that's possible," Phillip responded, trying to sound casual despite his eagerness.

Jim said, "I think we can make that happen under the following conditions. First, the parents have to know there will be drinking. Second, once everyone is here, I get their car keys. And third, you clean up any mess you make."

Art invited two of his classmates, plus Dawson, who was also home on leave from the Navy.

Phillip invited Mullinix, Rodney, and Max. Anna fixed finger sandwiches and other snacks, and Art picked up some pizza from George's. The basement was transformed for the party with lights and Art's portable boom box. They enjoyed their evening playing cards, talking about old times, laughing at inside jokes, and of course drinking a few beers. The room was filled with friends who had known each other forever but were now walking different paths.

It was just around 1:30 AM when everyone found a spot and crashed. Bodies were sprawled across sleeping bags on the basement floor.

Raymond tried not to trip over anyone when he got home a little later.

At about 3:00 AM, Jim was awakened by a ruckus coming from the bathroom. He rolled out of bed, opened the door, and there stood Phillip in his t-shirt and boxers, squinting at the bathtub.

"What's up?" Jim asked, rubbing sleep from his eyes.

"Oh hey, Pops," Phillip said, trying very hard to sound sober. "I can't seem to find the damn door to get out of here and back to bed." He gestured helplessly at the shower curtain as if it were an impassable barrier.

Jim stifled a laugh, helping him back into his own bed. Anna rolled over and sleepily asked what all that commotion was about.

Jim laughed and said, "Apparently Phillip got lost in the bathroom and asked 'Pops' for help. The poor kid was trying to exit through the bathtub."

Anna turned back over and said, "Well, they still have to clean up any mess they made, 'Pops,'" laughing to herself as she pulled the covers up. "That's the beauty of being the parents—we get to make the rules, they get to deal with the hangovers."

Chapter 16: Treasure Island

Orders arrived just after Christmas for Art and Phillip, directing them to report to Treasure Island, the naval base perched in the San Francisco Bay, by January 13, 1970. There, they would complete their dream sheets—preference forms that might shape their naval destinies—and await assignment to their next posts. This island served as a common launching point for reservists beginning their two-year active-duty commitments. Both were filled with anticipation at the prospect of their next naval journey, and one last adventure as brothers before going separate ways.

Upon arrival at the San Francisco airport, Art and Phillip were taken aback by the number of people rushing in every direction and the number of service members carrying duffel bags and seabags to destinations only known to them. The terminal hummed with activity—announcements echoed through the vast space, travelers rushed to make connections, and families reunited in emotional embraces.

It was the boys' first visit to the Bay Area, or any large city. Art looked at Phillip and said, "I didn't expect it to be this chaotic," as a hurried businessman nearly collided with them. The air was thick with the scents of coffee shops and fast food.

As they got closer to the baggage claim area, Phillip noticed a group of people with shaved heads wearing white robes standing in a semi-circle, beating on hand drums while chanting words he couldn't understand. They were drawing curious glances from passersby.

Art nodded toward them. "What do you think they're doing?"

Phillip studied the group with measured curiosity. "Not sure, but I assume they're protesting something."

A young woman approached them, "Would you like to learn about spiritual enlightenment through cosmic harmony?" she asked, extending a colorful pamphlet.

Phillip politely declined with a shake of his head. "We're just passing through, thanks."

As they moved toward the carousel, the baggage claim lurched to life with a mechanical groan, and the first pieces of luggage began to emerge from behind the rubber flaps.

Phillip grabbed his seabag and said, "Welcome to San Francisco."

They looked out the window as they crossed the Bay Bridge over to the island, noticing the iconic symbol of the city—the Golden Gate Bridge—standing majestically in the distance. Art pressed his face against the glass like an excited child, taking in the panoramic view of San Francisco's skyline.

"Would you look at that," he whispered, almost to himself. "Nothing like this back in Iowa."

They pulled into the naval facility on Treasure Island, the driver navigating through security checkpoints with practiced ease, coming to a stop in front of a weathered administrative building bearing the Navy insignia.

"This is it, gentlemen," the driver announced, turning to face them. "Welcome to your new temporary home."

Upon arrival, they walked into the administration office, where the smell of old paper and industrial cleaning supplies hung in the air. A yeoman behind the counter glanced up at them, his face a mask of practiced indifference cultivated through processing countless new arrivals.

"Orders," he said simply, extending his hand.

189

Art and Phillip handed the yeoman their papers. The office bustled with activity. The walls were lined with bulletin boards covered in notices, regulations, and faded photographs of naval vessels.

The yeoman looked over their papers, his expression revealing nothing. After what felt like an eternity, he reached beneath the counter and produced several documents.

"Here," he said, looking up to confirm their identities. "Here's your barracks assignment, Building C, third floor."

He also handed them a map of Treasure Island, a map of San Francisco, and a list showing what's off-limits if they planned on visiting the city. "Study it carefully. The Shore Patrol doesn't accept ignorance as an excuse."

Art nodded earnestly while Phillip took the documents, folding them carefully before tucking them into his pocket.

Then they were handed a paper with "Personnel Assignment Preferences" printed at the top.

"Dream sheet," the yeoman explained with the hint of a smile. "Pick three options or write in three and get it back to me by 0800 tomorrow at the latest. The sooner the better. Mess hall closes at 1900 hours," he added. "You'll find it marked on your map."

They made their way over to the barracks, a three-story concrete structure with windows that had been painted over too many times to count. They found two unclaimed lower bunks in a corner of the large room and stored their gear in the adjacent lockers.

They started looking over the dream sheet, sitting on their respective bunks. Art tapped his pen against his teeth as he considered the options.

"What are you thinking?" Phillip asked.

"Somewhere warm," Art replied. He circled Joint Base Pearl Harbor Hickam in Hawaii and Naval Air Station North Island in California with decisive strokes. Then, after a moment's hesitation, he wrote in "Vietnam" in the third space

Phillip raised an eyebrow. "Vietnam? Seriously? You trying to get yourself killed?"

Art shrugged. "Just want to go where the action is. Make a difference, you know? What about you, playing it safe as usual?"

Phillip ignored the jab and methodically selected the Naval Medical Center San Diego and the Naval Medical Center Portsmouth. After considering his third choice, he penciled in "Ship" with neat, block letters.

"A ship. Sea duty?" Art scoffed.

"Why be in the Navy and be landlocked?" Phillip replied. "Besides, I hear medical personnel on ships usually get better quarters."

They walked back over to the admin building and dropped their sheets off with the Yeoman, who barely looked up as he took the papers.

"Check the bulletin board each morning for your assignments," he instructed without breaking his typing rhythm. "If your names aren't on the list, you have the rest of that day to yourselves. If you see your name, come back in here for orders, transportation vouchers, and per diem."

As they stepped back outside, the late afternoon sun was setting over the cityscape across the bay. Naval personnel moved purposefully across the grounds, some in working uniforms, others dressed for liberty in the city.

"So," Art said, unfolding the map of San Francisco. "We've got one night before everything changes. What do you think? Should we see what this city has to offer?"

Phillip shook his head. "I doubt they'll have any assignments for us that soon. I was thinking of calling it a day, getting some chow, and heading back. I'm exhausted.

According to Iowa time, it's 1900, not 1600 hours."

Art agreed with a nod. "Let's wait until tomorrow when it's daylight. But let's try to stay out of trouble. I didn't come all this way to get a captain's mast before my first assignment."

Phillip grinned. "I'll try, but I make no promises."

The next morning, after breakfast, they went over to check the bulletin board. After a careful examination, Art said, "I don't see anything."

Phillip turned to Art. "You want to stay in uniform or change?"

Art answered, "Hell, they know we're in the service by our haircuts. Let's change."

They grabbed a city bus going to South Market Street. The ride took about half an hour across the Bay Bridge. Once in the city, they started walking around. The hills were immediately noticeable, creating dramatic views and a unique urban landscape. The city's location on the bay offered stunning water views, adding to its visual appeal. San Francisco was known for its diverse population, which contributed to its vibrant and eclectic atmosphere. Getting around was simple—ride the cable car, trolley, or catch a

193

bus—perfect for first-time visitors.

Now, the only problem was where they had gotten off. Phillip noticed it was marked on the map as "off limits." They were in the Tenderloin district of San Francisco, historically bounded by Geary Street to the north, Market Street to the south, Mason Street to the east, and Van Ness Avenue to the west. The area encompassed about fifty square blocks and was situated between the Union Square shopping district and the Civic Center office district. It was off-limits because of high crime, drugs, and prostitution. They jumped on another bus and headed down to Fisherman's Wharf.

As they rode down the hill, they went past the colorful and ornate Victorian houses, like the Painted Ladies, a distinct feature of the city's character. Their vibrant colors and intricate designs stood out against the clear blue sky, capturing the essence of San Francisco's unique architectural heritage.

As they got closer to the waterfront, they caught their first look at Alcatraz Island. Initially used as a military fortress to protect the city, it later served as a military prison for holding offenders during World War II, and finally as a maximum-security prison for the nation's most dangerous criminals. It once housed infamous inmates like Al Capone,

George "Machine-Gun" Kelly, and Alvin Karpis, the first "Public Enemy Number One." But today, it was being occupied by Native Americans who had taken over in 1969, claiming Alcatraz Island as Indian Land.

The bus wound its way down to the waterfront, where the smell of salt air and fresh seafood filled their nostrils. It was bustling with activity—vendors called out their wares, and tourists from around the world mingled in the city by the Bay. Phillip checked his map again, relieved to be in a more welcoming part of the city.

"This is more like it," Phillip said, folding the map and tucking it into his back pocket. "I think we're safe here.

The sea lions at Pier 39 barked loudly in the distance, as if welcoming everyone to San Francisco. The afternoon stretched before them, full of possibilities.

The boys walked around and took in the sounds and smells of this magical place. The salty air mixed with the aroma of fresh seafood and sourdough bread baking in nearby bakeries.

"You hungry?" asked Art, eyeing the numerous food stalls lining the waterfront.

"Sure," said Phillip, patting his stomach. "Have you ever

known a time I couldn't eat?"

They stopped at one of the crab shops, its counters displaying heaps of freshly caught seafood on beds of ice. The vendor recommended the boys try the fresh clam chowder served in a sourdough bread bowl.

"Best in San Francisco," the vendor proclaimed with a proud smile as he handed over their orders.

They grabbed a bowl each and found a place to sit along the pier. The chowder was creamy and rich, with tender clams and chunks of potato, and the sourdough bowl added a flavor that complemented the soup perfectly.

They ate and watched people walking around in no particular hurry, tourists and locals alike enjoying the pleasant day. Seagulls circled overhead, occasionally swooping down when someone dropped a morsel of food.

As they finished eating the last of the bread, Phillip leaned back contentedly. "I could get used to this."

Art wiped away the last evidence of the food from his mouth with a napkin and said, "Now, where do you want to go?"

Phillip pulled out his map and pointed to a USO club

back up the hill. "Let's go here. Maybe they can guide us to places we might want to see."

They jumped back on a cable car, gripping the poles as it began its climb up the steep San Francisco streets. Holding on tightly, Phillip started singing, "Rice-A-Roni, the San Francisco Treat." The riders broke out laughing and then collectively joined in for one more chorus, followed by the driver ringing the bell, the impromptu sing-along creating a moment of connection among the strangers.

They rode through downtown San Francisco, getting off at the Embarcadero in front of the Ferry Building, its clock tower standing tall against the sky. They spotted the USO sign just a short distance away and walked the few steps to it, hoping to find some local knowledge about the best places for young sailors to visit in the city by the Bay.

Everywhere they looked, they saw service members from every branch. Some in uniform, but most, like them, wearing civvies. There were girls from a local college there, probably to get away from their studies and just relax in a safe place. Phillip and Art sat watching, drinking coffee.

"You going to ask one of those girls to dance?" Art asked.

"Not tonight," answered Phillip. That is, until a Santana song started to play through the speakers, and then he was up. Something about the song "Evil Ways" pulled him from his seat. Art watched as his usually reserved brother made his way to the dance floor.

A young brunette with a bright smile caught Phillip's eye. He gestured toward the dance floor, where she joined him.

Art sipped his coffee and checked his watch—they'd been there longer than planned, as he saw the fading sun outside.

When the song ended, Art signaled to Phillip that they needed to get back before dark. The base was a good thirty-minute ride, and things looked different after dark.

After three bus transfers, they were back at the barracks, where they sat and talked about their day.

"Where did you find that move you were doing on the dance floor?" asked Art.

Phillip got up to duplicate it. "Like it? I saw it on American Bandstand."

"Not a fan," Art responded, laughing.

198

The next morning, the routine was the same. Breakfast at 0700 and then walk over to the admin office to check the bulletin board. As they made their way across the base, Art said, "Maybe today." His voice carried a mixture of hope and nervousness.

When they reached the board, Art found his name. He would be going to Naval Air Station Bermuda. Phillip scanned the list and found his own name—he would be attached to the USS Midway, currently at Hunter's Point Naval Shipyards.

"Well, you got your ship," Art said with a grin, clapping Phillip on the shoulder. "And I got some warm weather."

They walked into the admin office and again spoke with the yeoman, a meticulous petty officer who had been handling the transfer paperwork all week. He left his desk, went through some packets, and came back, handing both Phillip and Art theirs.

"Everything you need to know is in the packet," the yeoman said, sliding the manila envelopes across the counter. "If you need transport to the airport or to the shipyard, just call the number that's in your packet. Good luck!"

They thanked him and went back to their barracks to open their packets. Art flipped through his papers and announced, "I'm leaving tomorrow." He looked over at Phillip, who was still reading. "When do you report?"

"No later than January 18th," Phillip replied, then laughed. "I guess the Navy is giving me three whole days to go across the Bay Bridge?" Hunter's Point was just outside of San Francisco, barely a thirty-minute drive from where they were.

After putting everything in their lockers, Art turned to Phillip and said, "You feel like one more day in the city?"

"Sure," Phillip responded, already reaching for his wallet. "I need to get some of that famous sourdough bread. And we deserve one last outing before we go our separate ways."

Art nodded, understanding the unspoken sentiment. They had spent almost their entire life together, but tomorrow that was going to change.

They headed toward the bus stop, their conversation filled with plans for the day. The morning fog was just beginning to burn off, revealing patches of blue sky above the city's rolling hills. This time they took Bus #28 to 19th and stayed on until they reached the Golden Gate Bridge, its magnificent orange towers emerging dramatically from the thinning mist over the bay.

They spent the day sightseeing, relaxing, and just enjoying their last day together. They shared a sourdough bread bowl filled with clam chowder, laughing as seagulls eyed their meal with obvious interest. The knowledge that tomorrow would separate them hung in the background, making each moment feel both precious and bittersweet. Jumping on the Powell Street cable car, they started their descent to the wharf. The car stopped to pick up a couple more passengers, and both Art and Phillip gave up their seats, preferring to stand holding onto the rail. They had their backs turned as they looked back to where they had come from when a car tried to cross the tracks, getting broadsided by the cable car.

Both Art and Phillip fell to the ground. After lying there for a moment, they stood up to see what had happened. Both were fine, but a police officer still had to take their information for his report, telling them someone might get in touch with them later if they needed any more information.

It wasn't far to the wharf, so they decided to walk the rest of the way. Art complained his wrist hurt a little bit, so Phillip looked at it and, after gently testing it, said, "I think it's just a sprain, but watch to see if there's any swelling. If so, you may need to have it x-rayed."

Art responded jokingly, "It's nice having a doc nearby."

The day gave way to early evening, so they decided to head back so they could write letters home telling their parents where they would be going, pack, and get ready for tomorrow. Art's flight was almost nine hours with a layover in Philadelphia. Adding that to the time change of four hours, it was going to be a very long day.

The morning came too quickly. Art was meticulously putting on his dress whites while Phillip, who didn't need to pack yet, sat on his bunk watching. The barracks were quiet except for the occasional sound of other sailors preparing for the day. Sunlight filtered through the windows, casting long rectangles of light across the floor.

"I bet the weather in Bermuda is going to be a lot warmer than here," Phillip said, breaking the silence that had grown between them.

Art nodded as he adjusted his collar in the small mirror hanging in his locker. "Yeah, that's why I'm wearing the whites instead of the blues," he replied while shoving his pea coat into his seabag. His movements were deliberate but tinged with an underlying nervousness. This was it—the first major step in his naval career, and he was taking it alone.

Phillip watched his brother pack, mentally cataloging each item as if trying to fix this moment in his memory. They had shared a bedroom back in Iowa for seventeen years, and now they were heading to opposite corners of the world.

"You got everything?" Phillip asked, reaching for Art's cover that had fallen to the floor. He handed it to his brother, their fingers briefly touching during the exchange.

"Think so," Art replied, taking one last look around the barracks space that had been his home for the past few days.

"Mom's going to worry."

"Mom always worries," Phillip said with a small smile. "That's her job."

Art picked up his bag and sat down on the edge of his bunk. "Remember when we were kids and I broke my arm falling out of the couch? She didn't leave my side for three days."

Phillip laughed. "Yeah, and when you finally went back to school, she made me walk you to every class even though we were in different grades."

"She's going to be even worse now that we're both gone," Art said, his smile fading slightly.

"Dad will keep her busy," Phillip assured him. "And we'll write. You better write, you know."

Art nodded and glanced at his watch. "The transport will be here any minute."

Phillip stood up, clearing his throat. "You know, I've been thinking. We don't have to lose touch just because we're in different places."

Art stood and grabbed his seabag, slinging it over his shoulder. The movement was smooth, practiced—they had been trained well.

Suddenly, the naval bearing they'd been taught seemed to create an invisible barrier between them, as if they were already becoming different people.

"I should go," Art said, his voice taking on a formality that hadn't been there moments before.

They walked together through the barracks and out into the crisp morning air. A military transport vehicle was idling at the curb, its driver leaning against the hood, smoking a cigarette. A few other sailors were already inside, their faces obscured by the glare on the windows.

"Well, this is it," Art said as he turned toward the waiting transport. He hesitated, then set down his bag and extended his hand formally.

Phillip looked at the outstretched hand and then pulled his brother into a hug instead. After a moment's resistance, Art embraced him back, tightly. They stood there, frozen in time, neither wanting to be the first to let go.

"Take care of yourself, little brother," Art said, his voice rough with emotion.

They pulled apart, both blinking rapidly in the morning sunlight. Art picked up his bag and turned toward the transport. Halfway there, he looked back over his shoulder. "I'll send you my address as soon as I get settled."

"You better," Phillip called back, trying to keep his voice light. "And don't go falling for the first pretty girl you see in Bermuda."

Art grinned. "No promises."

With that, he boarded the transport. The door closed behind him with a solid thunk that seemed to echo across the base. As the vehicle pulled away, Phillip raised his hand in a final farewell, not knowing if Art could see him through the tinted windows.

Phillip stood there long after the transport had disappeared from view. The base continued its morning routine around him—sailors heading to breakfast, officers striding purposefully toward administrative buildings.

He knew the special bond they had shared was probably not going to be the same after today. They would be worlds away from each other and likely wouldn't see each other for the next two years. The realization hit him with unexpected force. They had never been separated for more than a few weeks before.

They were growing into men and would need to pursue their paths without each other. The thought was both terrifying and oddly liberating. For the first time, Phillip wouldn't be known as "one of the McManus' boys" but simply as himself.

Back in the barracks, he sat on his bunk, looking at Art's stripped mattress. He pulled out his own paperwork and began reviewing it, focusing on the details of his assignment. The familiar routine of studying information helped steady him.

Later that afternoon, Phillip caught himself turning to share something with Art, only to find empty space. It was a small moment, but it underscored the magnitude of the change happening in his life.

As he sealed the envelope, Phillip made a silent promise to himself. They might be pursuing separate lives now, but they would always be brothers—a bond that not even the Navy could break.

Chapter 17 : USS Midway

Phillip grew tired of sitting in a lonely barracks and decided he would head over to his ship. The orders said no later than January 18th, so he suspected any time would be fine. He picked up the base phone and asked if they could send a vehicle to his barracks so he could get over to Hunter's Point. The sailor on the other end said it would be thirty or forty minutes before he could get a ride. That gave Phillip more than enough time to get his gear packed.

The military sedan arrived out front, and Phillip headed out the door, taking one look back before throwing his sea bag in the back seat. He climbed in the front saying, "I'm ready."

"Hunter's Point?" the seaman asked.

"Yep. I guess my ship isn't ready to sail, but it's ready for me," Phillip responded.

There was small talk as they headed over the Bay Bridge. Once they crossed, the driver took a hard left into the shipyard. After about a mile, the car came to a stop.

"This is as far as I can go," the driver told Phillip.

Phillip looked up at the monster in front of him and wondered how in the hell it floated. He grabbed his bag from the back seat, put on his cover, and started the long walk to the gangway that led aboard. It was over a quarter mile walk, something Phillip had done many times before, but never carrying a fifty-pound sea bag.

Phillip recalled all he had read about the Midway as he made his way aft. She weighed just under seventy thousand tons, stood ten stories tall, was over eleven hundred feet long, and now, with the angled deck, just under three hundred feet wide. She would be home for around five thousand sailors, including the air crew. Three stories of the ten were below the waterline. She had two large elevators to move aircraft from the hangar deck to the flight deck and could hold over one hundred and twenty planes.

The ship was first going to be a battleship, but in 1946, the war was over in Europe, and they switched to make her a flat top for the Pacific. Named after the Battle of Midway.

The attack aircraft carrier Midway (CVA-41) was scheduled to be recommissioned on 31 January 1970 and ready for sea duty by early 1971, having undergone the most comprehensive modernization ever undertaken by the Navy. She became the largest and most modern carrier in her class.

As Phillip came aboard, he turned left, saluted the Union Jack, and then the officer, again saluting and saying, "Permission to come aboard." He set down his bag, handed his orders to the lieutenant, and waited. As the officer picked up the phone to call someone to come get him, Phillip started looking at this magnificent giant he would be calling home.

Soon, he heard a sailor say, "McManus, follow me." He thought he recognized the voice, and when he looked in the direction of the voice, he was surprised and pleased to see Martinez standing there with a big smile.

"Grab your bag, Corpsman, and let me show you your new living quarters."

They walked the hangar deck, trying to avoid all the construction equipment and civilians who were busy bringing life back to this ship. They reached a hatch going below, and Martinez showed him the best way down. He put his arms on the metal handrails, picked up his feet, and slid.

"Throw me your bag and come on."

Phillip tossed his bag and slid down, thinking that was a fast way to go below. Once below, they walked through hatches they called "knee knockers," where you had to step over while ducking your head to clear. Phillip instantly recalled the movies where sailors would be trapped as some closed and sealed them to prevent the ship from taking on water. Martinez saw the concern in Phillip's eyes and said, "This ship isn't going to sink." Apparently, he had seen the same movies.

Once they reached the berthing area, Carlos said, "Pick a rack. I got this one, but if you want, you can have the one above mine."

The racks were three high, and the middle was perfect, never having to bend over to get things out. Phillip stowed most of his gear in the space once Carlos showed him how to access it by lifting up his bed. The uniforms that needed to be hung up were placed in a small wall locker.

"They didn't expect you until tomorrow. So change into your dungarees. Here's a ball cap, and let me show you around before introducing you to our medical crew."

They walked the ship from bow to stern, upstairs, downstairs, finding the mess hall, the ship's stores, laundry, bridge, flight deck, and finally, sick bay—all the places Phillip would need while aboard. The mess hall was open for all three meals and, once at sea, twenty-three hours a day, because there were always sailors awake and working when the ship was at sea.

As the tour concluded, Phillip felt both overwhelmed and excited. The Midway wasn't just a ship—it was a floating city, a marvel of engineering, and now his home. Carlos clapped him on the shoulder. "Glad we will be serving together."

They made their way to sick bay, where several medical personnel were busy organizing supplies. The chief medical officer, Lieutenant Commander Adams, was overlooking paperwork when Carlos brought Phillip in.

"Sir," Carlos said. "This is our new corpsman, McManus."

The commander looked up, steel-gray eyes examining Phillip from head to toe. "You're early, McManus. Good. Shows initiative."

He stood and extended his hand. "I've reviewed your file, and Martinez told me about your time at A school. You will be a good fit on this team. We're glad to have you."

"Thank you, sir. Eager to serve," Phillip replied, surprised the officer had taken time to learn about him.

Showing him the medical facility, Carlos said, "We've got

a twenty-bed ward, two operating rooms, x-ray machines, a lab, pharmacy, and even dental facilities," he explained. "When you're on a floating city with thousands of men, you need to be prepared for anything."

They passed through a room where several corpsmen were talking. One of them, a thin man with wire-rimmed glasses, looked up.

"Hey, this the new guy?"

"Yeah, McManus, meet Jenkins. Pharmacist's mate."

Jenkins grinned. "Welcome!"

After completing the tour of the medical facilities, they headed to the mess hall for dinner. The large space was bustling with sailors, the clatter of trays and hum of conversation filling the air. The food was better than Phillip expected—roast beef, mashed potatoes, and green beans.

After dinner, they returned to their berthing area, where Phillip continued organizing his personal space. Other sailors began filtering in, each one stopping to introduce themselves to the newcomer. By lights out, Phillip had met nearly everyone in his section.

As he lay in his rack that night, he tried to comprehend

what his new life was going to look like. Tomorrow, he would officially report for duty, but tonight he was already home. The Midway would soon carry him across the vast Pacific to places he'd only read about. As he drifted off to sleep, Phillip wondered what adventures awaited him aboard this floating city of steel.

The next morning came early with the sound of a boatswain's whistle over the PA system.

"Reveille, reveille. All hands turn, too. The smoking lamp is lit in all designated smoking areas."

Phillip sat up quickly, nearly hitting his head on the rack above. Around him, sailors were already moving, some heading to the showers, others quickly making their racks with practiced efficiency.

"Morning, Doc," Carlos called from below. "Sleep well?"

"Like a baby," Phillip lied, not wanting to admit he'd tossed and turned half the night.

"Good. Because today's going to be a long one."

After a quick breakfast, Phillip and Martinez reported to sick bay.

"McManus, good. I am Chief Mitchell, and today you're

going to be a fire watch. Martinez will show you the ropes."

Phillips stood in the shadowy depths of the carrier's hull, assigned to trail civilian welders as they fused massive steel joints and reinforced vital sections of the ship. His orders were clear: stay vigilant, fire extinguisher in hand, ready to douse any errant sparks before they could ignite into something more dangerous. As he peered through the protective welding helmet they'd issued him—its glass shield darkening with each brilliant flash—Phillips couldn't suppress his frustration. After all those grueling months of naval training, countless drills and exercises, his first real assignment amounted to playing babysitter to civilian contractors.

Gradually, despite his initial disappointment, Phillips found himself mesmerized by the transformation unfolding before him. The civilians, whom he'd initially regarded with thinly veiled disdain, turned out to be skilled craftsmen whose expertise he came to respect. They shared stories of other ships they'd helped build or repair, offering Phillips a different perspective on naval service than what he'd learned in training.

After weeks of ten-hour shifts, sweat-soaked uniforms, and the constant symphony of industrial noise, recommissioning day finally arrived. Every member of the ship's company stood at attention on the flight deck, dress uniforms pressed and spotless, as the vessel was ceremonially transferred to its new commander. Captain Carol approached the podium with confident strides, his voice carrying clearly across the assembly as he accepted command and outlined his vision for their upcoming deployment.

In just a few more weeks, this massive carrier was scheduled to slip its moorings and emerge from dry dock, gliding across the calm waters to its new home at Alameda Naval Air Station, just across the bay. Phillips could hardly wait to see her on the water, no longer a construction site but a formidable warship—one that, in some small way, he had helped bring back to life.

That evening, liberty passes were being issued for the first time since they'd boarded. They were free to escape the ship with the instructions that they had to be back aboard the ship by 0700.

"A few hours of freedom," Carlos said, tucking his pass into his wallet. "What should we do first?"

"Anything that doesn't involve following orders or smelling like welders' smoke," Phillip replied,

Bryan Wilson, a lanky kid from Morro Bay, California, with sun-bleached hair, had already plotted their evening.

"Let's start at the USO first," he announced, slapping Phillip on the shoulder. "I hear it is the best spot to start." They've got decent coffee, sometimes food, and most importantly—" he paused for dramatic effect, "—people to talk to who don't smell like the inside of an engine room or have Adam's apples."

The three of them stood at the ship's gangway, saluting as protocol demanded before heading to the gate where they could catch a city bus. They navigated the unfamiliar streets with the help of a crumpled map Phillip still had until they spotted the red, white, and blue USO sign. They entered, hoping for the promise of normal conversation and civilian faces with lipstick.

As they pushed open the door, the sound of laughter and music washed over them.

They navigated through the packed USO club. The scent of coffee mingled with perfume and aftershave as service members from across the country sought a few hours of normalcy.

Through a stroke of luck, they spotted an unclaimed

table in the corner. They quickly claimed it, setting down their cups of coffee, hastily assembled sandwiches, and a small napkin.

They watched as young women and servicemen talked and danced. The overhead lights cast a warm glow while the band played current hits that momentarily drowned out thoughts of military duties.

Phillip spotted a girl standing alone near the edge of the dance floor. She held a soda glass with both hands, occasionally taking small sips. There was something about her that caught Phillip's eye.

"Why don't you go ask her to dance?" Wilson's voice cut through Phillip's thoughts.

"What?" Phillip leaned closer, the bass from the speakers making conversation nearly impossible. Wilson rolled his eyes and pointed in her direction.

"Her. Go. Dance." He mouthed the words with exaggerated clarity.

Phillip hesitated, but something about tonight—maybe the rare evening of freedom, maybe the three cups of coffee—gave him a surge of boldness.

'The worst that could happen is she says no,' he thought to himself. 'And in this crowd, we'd probably never cross paths again anyway.'

Before his courage could falter, he stood up and made his way across the room until he reached her side.

"Hello," he said, raising his voice just enough to be heard over the music. "I'm Phillip. Would you like to dance?"

"I'd love to," she replied, placing her glass on a nearby table.

They had barely stepped on the dance floor when the fast-paced song ended, the final notes fading before the first haunting chords of "House of the Rising Sun" by The Animals filled the room. Phillip hesitated, one foot already retreating toward the sidelines.

"I'm not ready to sit down," she said. "Are you?"

"Not at all," Phillip answered, gently placing his hands at her waist as she rested hers on his shoulders.

As they danced, they exchanged the basics. Her name was Charlie.

"Charlotte, actually, but nobody calls me that except my grandmother," she explained with a laugh. "I'm from Kauai," she told him. "But I'm here at the University of San Francisco, Sophomore year, in nursing."

Phillip couldn't help but laugh. "You're kidding? I just finished my medical corpsman training. Looks like we're both going to be patching people up."

She was petite, the top of her head barely reaching his chin. Her black hair, glossy under the club's lights, fell just to her shoulders, the ends turning under slightly. Her complexion was a warm, light brown, and her dark eyes reflected both intelligence and warmth.

But it was more than her physical beauty that held Phillip captivated. There was an openness to her expression, a genuine curiosity when she asked him questions about his training and hometown. Charlie's authenticity was magnetic.

And when the song ended and another began, neither made any move to leave the dance floor.

The night had slipped away faster than any of them expected. The USO volunteer behind the refreshment counter had already begun wiping down surfaces, a gentle but clear signal that closing time approached.

"I should probably go," he finally said, nodding toward Carlos and Wilson, who were hovering near the exit, "My buddies are waiting."

Charlie brushed away a strand of hair from her face and smiled. "I had a really nice time tonight."

"Me too," he said. "Maybe I'll see you around again sometime?" The question hung on the surface but was weighted with hope.

"I'm usually here on Fridays," she said, gathering her purse. "It's my escape from nursing textbooks and anatomy charts. One night a week, where I don't have to think about bodily systems and medication."

With a warm smile and hopes of meeting again, the two departed. Phillip rejoined his shipmates, and the trio of sailors stepped out into the cool night air, the contrast between the warm club and the San Francisco chill making them walk faster toward the bus stop.

"Did you get her number?" Carlos asked the moment they were out of earshot, bumping his shoulder against Phillip's with brotherly familiarity.

Phillip shook his head. "Well, no. What am I supposed to call her on, the ship's phone?" He attempted a laugh, but it came out hollow. "Or maybe walk down to the end of the pier and call, hoping she'll be there waiting by some miracle?" He paused, hands deep in his pockets to keep them warm.

"She said she's usually there on Fridays," he added.

Wilson's face broke into a knowing grin. "So, she wants to see you again."

"Maybe," Phillip replied, his tone noncommittal. They fell silent as they boarded the crowded bus heading back to Hunters Point, squeezing themselves into the last available seats among other sailors.

As the bus lurched forward, its headlights cutting through the fog that had begun to settle over the city, Phillip leaned his head against the window. The vibration of the glass against his head created a strange counterpoint to his thoughts, which kept circling back to Charlie. He replayed the moments from their evening—her hand in his as they danced, the way she'd leaned in closer to hear him over the music, how her eyes had crinkled at the corners when she laughed at his clumsy jokes.

There was something different about her, something he couldn't quite name. It wasn't just her looks, though he found her captivating. It wasn't just her intelligence; it was something in the way she seemed fully present in each moment, genuinely interested in his stories about his hometown in Iowa. Maybe it was just the time, and tonight they just needed to escape whatever was on their minds. In a world where everyone seemed to be changing, they had found a moment to just get away from it all and have some fun.

As the bus turned the corner, carrying them back to the ship that would soon become their floating home for months to come, Phillip knew with unexpected clarity that he wanted to spend more time with Charlie. Even if it meant navigating the uncertainty of a connection, he had no idea where it would take him.

The realization both excited and terrified him. Nothing in his training had prepared him for the unpredictable territories of the heart, for wanting something he couldn't chart on a map or secure with proper protocol.

Beside him, Carlos and Wilson had already moved on to discussing their plans for their next liberty, but Phillip was still lost in her dark eyes and gentle hands. He wondered when they'd meet next.

'Maybe we can go somewhere and have a coffee away from the crowds, noise, and just get to know each other a little better,' he thought, setting his head against the cool window glass, not knowing that wide smile was plastered on his face all this time.

Chapter 18 : Mooring Lines: Life Aboard the Never Float

The days were busy finishing the last items necessary for the ship to move over to Alameda. After a 4-month delay due to labor disputes, design changes, and material shortages, the construction equipment was finally being removed, cranes pulled away, and civilians who had completed their mission walked off the ship for the last time.

The ship was pushed out into the harbor by a couple of tugs, and the Harbor Captain steered her out, giving up control to the helmsman. A trip that was scheduled for late February was now getting underway in May. The ship made a slow, steady pace as it was underway. Passing Alcatraz, slipping under the Bay Bridge, and avoiding other traffic in the bay. Soon, another tug came out and started pushing this bigger-than-life ship into her resting spot on Pier 22.

Ropes were flung over the side to awaiting ship handlers who secured her to the pier using strong mooring lines that were carefully placed and tightened, ensuring that the ship would be stationary despite weather or rising tides.

The sailors, who had no responsibility for moving the ship, watched from the flight deck. A gentle but cool breeze was blowing in their hair as they secured their work jackets up to their chins, keeping the wet breeze out. Some walked around, others took pictures. Phillip looked out at Alcatraz and asked Chief Mitchell if that was a teepee on the island. The chief looked out, saying, "It sure is. I haven't seen one of those since I left New Mexico."

Wilson and Martinez were standing closer to the edge with Doctor Davis, a surgeon from Indiana who had just come aboard. They were looking down over the safety nets, which were there to stop a sailor who might fall over the side or get blown off by back blast from a jet, thinking about how far that drop would be if they had to abandon ship. Martinez said it is a good thing these ships don't sink because that jump would kill you.

Commander Davis, whose first duty was on the Forrestal back in 1967, said, "It almost happened on July 29, 1967, while in the Tonkin Gulf in Vietnam, when an electrical anomaly caused a Zuni rocket on an F-4B Phantom to fire, striking external fuel tanks on an A-4 Skyhawk causing a chain of fires. When it was finally out, there were 134 sailors dead and another 161 injured, some would be scarred for life. The ship survived, but the damages took her off line with an estimated damage of over seventy-two million dollars."

The commander looked at Martinez with cold eyes and said, "We were lucky that day. It could have been worse, and what you said about jumping wouldn't have even been a concern to some, as they made the plunge to avoid the heat and fire."

As they passed under the Bay Bridge, Wilson yelled out, "We fit!"

The chief laughed and said, "Yeah, the Navy already knew that answer. Now let's get below. We have a lot of work to do once we get docked before we call it a day."

The day went by quickly, and it was time for evening chow. Martinez, Wilson, and Johansen—a big Swedish boy from Minnesota—headed down for dinner. As they walked through the line getting their trays filled, Phillip sighed.

"Roast beef again?" he grumbled.

"Just wait," Manu said with a knowing smile. He was also assigned to the medical group as a Second-Class Petty Officer and was from Hawaii. "You'll be dreaming of beef once we get going."

After dinner, they checked the duty roster to see who had evening duty. Johansen stretched his long arms overhead and asked if anyone felt like heading to the post bowling alley for a few games and a couple of beers. Phillip perked up—he hadn't bowled since he was in a youth league back at Leo's bowling alley in Ottumwa.

"Let's go," Wilson said, already heading toward the exit.

They stayed in their dungarees and headed back to disembark. It was a long walk from where the ship was docked to the main post. Finally arriving, they got their shoes and settled down in an alley.

"Who wants to go first?" asked Martinez, lacing up his bowling shoes.

"I can show you the way," Wilson boasted as he picked up his ball and flung it down the lane.

"Damn," Martinez chuckled. "I thought you were supposed to roll it, not toss it."

Everyone erupted in laughter while Wilson, not appreciating the ribbing, defended himself, "I got my thumb stuck!"

After a few games and a few beers, they figured they

needed to head back. As they were walking along the waterfront, a blue sedan flew past them, and before anyone could shout a warning, it shot off the deck and plunged into the bay.

"Holy shit!" yelled Phillip, eyes wide with shock.

They ran to where the car had entered the water. Two men were already out, swimming desperately toward the pier.

"Anyone still in the car?" Martinez shouted at the swimmers.

"One passed out in the back seat," one of them gasped.

Without hesitation, Johansen stripped off his jacket and jumped in, swimming down to the submerged car. Martinez, not being a good swimmer, stayed on top and helped the two men out of the water. Wilson and Phillip had climbed down and were helping pull the men up to Martinez.

"Got him!" came the call from the water.

They looked out and saw Johanson as he started swimming toward Phillip. The rescued passenger was awake and appeared to be fine, coughing up water, but conscious.

By the time they had everyone up, the Shore Patrol,

along with an ambulance, had arrived with their lights flashing.

"We got it from here," said the patrolman, taking over the scene.

They gave their statements to the Shore Patrol officer and started back to the ship, drenched and shivering in the night air.

Johansen ran a hand through his wet hair. "Well, this was an exciting day. I hope things get a little less exciting in the days to come."

Phillip piped up, a grin spreading across his face, "If anyone offers you a ride to the pier, may I suggest you say 'thanks' and keep walking?"

"No shit," said Martinez as he took off his shirt and wrung it out, water splashing onto the dock beneath their feet.

As they approached the gangway to their ship, their soaked clothes clinging to them, they knew they'd have a story to tell during tomorrow's shift—and perhaps a newfound respect from their crewmates. Not many sailors could say their evening at the bowling alley ended with a heroic rescue.

The ship was a mess after the construction crew left. It was fit for sailing, just not for living in. Floor tiles were scratched and dull. The dust was so thick, you could write your name in it. Ropes were missing, and some areas weren't even livable.

Each morning, the boatswain's mate would blow his whistle and announce over the PA system, "Sweepers, sweepers, man your brooms and clean the ship fore and aft." If your pay grade was E4 or below, that announcement was meant for you.

Strip the deck, wax the deck, and then buff it to a high shine. Once you were done, you would do it all over again because you were never really ready for inspection. Remove items, dust, store away goods and equipment. This daily routine was so tiresome that sailors started referring to their rates as "buffer mates" on the USS Never-Float.

The lower-ranked men formed an unspoken brotherhood of shared misery, exchanging knowing glances whenever the boatswain's whistle shrieked through the corridors.

"This isn't what I signed up for," muttered Wilson.

"Hell, I buff the same ten-foot stretch of hallway for the third time this week."

"Navy recruitment posters never show this part," Phillip agreed, wiping sweat from his brow as he applied another coat of wax to the floor outside the sick bay.

Chief Petty Officer Mitchell liked to remind them, "A clean ship is a happy ship, boys."

Phillip and Charlie were dating, often doubling with Carlos and another nursing student who was a close friend of Charlie's, named Renee. They went to the movies and held hands, splitting a Coke and a bag of popcorn, even stealing a kiss now and then. They were becoming more than just friends and were content with the time they shared. Where would it go? That wasn't even a question they were thinking about. For now, they were just what they both needed to interrupt the hectic life of school and service.

As winter turned to spring, their causal relationship evolved into longer conversations over coffee at the small cafés. Their conversations flowed effortlessly between serious discussions, like the recent shooting of protesters at Kent State, about their future careers and playful debates about whether pineapple belongs on pizza.

"You two are sickeningly cute," Renee whispered to Charlie one evening.

Charlie blushed but didn't deny it. The relationship was becoming an anchor in the stormy sea of exams, clinical rotations, and sleep-deprived study nights.

As they sat in Charlie's dorm room surrounded by pillows, rain pattering against the windows, Charlie realized that what had started as casual dating had grown into something neither had anticipated but both now cherished. They weren't rushing to define it or map out its future. For now, in this moment with fingers intertwined and comfortable silence between them, they were exactly where they needed to be.

Charlie went home to Hawaii once school was out for the year. As she stepped off the plane, the scent of plumeria welcomed her back to the islands. She would not be returning to the mainland until early September, and those summer months were a welcome relief from school.

She wrote to Phillip regularly, her letters filled with tales of morning swims in turquoise waters, family dinners on the lanai with her grandmother, and the sunsets that had to be seen to be appreciated. "The sunsets here make me miss you more," she wrote in one letter.

Phillip kept her updated about life on the ship, detailing the boredom of naval routines. "The guys tease me for writing so often," he admitted in one letter, "but they're all jealous I have someone like you to write to."

He also kept in touch with his family back in Iowa. His letters home were more guarded, edited to remove the worries and small hardships that would only make his mother fret.

Raymond had gone to work for the city's fire department. And he was dating a friend of Phillip's from Walsh, whose brother had been killed in 1968 in Vietnam.

Art had turned twenty-one and was enjoying his time in Bermuda. Jim and Anna were adjusting to a house that seemed a little bigger with all their boys gone. They had converted one of the bedrooms into a family room, where it was a little cozier to watch TV.

Anna never expressed her concerns directly, but Phillip knew she was getting concerned about his deployment to Vietnam at the beginning of the year.

Often, at night, while Phillip lay awake in his bunk, he re-read the letters from Charlie, his parents, and brothers. Letters that connected him to all the separate lives continuing without him.

The ship they had come to refer to as the USS Never-

Float started to come to life, spending days at sea practicing the skills they were going to need once deployed. Aircraft from Alameda would fly out to test the proficiency of everyone responsible for recovering and launching the aircraft. Phillip, along with other corpsmen, stood on the flight deck observing these operations and learning the types of injuries they might need to handle once they were underway. There would be three corpsmen assigned during every operation, and everyone needed to understand not just their duties but the dangers they would face on an active flight deck.

Planes performed touch-and-goes, while others missed the wire as the LSO yelled "Bolter!" in everyone's headset, advising the pilot to keep going and try again. They also got their sea legs, learning to move with the ship as it pitched and rolled, cutting through waves surfers could only dream of. They learned to put things away, latch things down, and never walk away from their food tray, because if you did, you'd be eating off the floor.

In September, Charlie returned to college. Phillip had marked his calendar for their planned reunion in San Francisco. Charlie wanted to take Phillip down to Ghirardelli Square and a special place she and Renee had discovered before heading home for the summer. It was called "The Little Wine Cellar." The servers were dressed like monks with their brown robes, or habits, as they liked to call them, with a rope around their waist and sandals on their feet. They served fresh fondue with sourdough bread chunks and wine, while guests listened to live folk music.

It was a magical place for sure, with one drawback. Charlie had celebrated her 21st birthday, but Phillip had not, and when carded, he had to ask for coffee, which Charlie said would be fine for her, too.

On Thanksgiving 1970, the families and guests of the crew were invited to come aboard. They had special passes to get them on base and transportation to get them down to the ship.

They got underway and as it approached the Bay Bridge and Golden Gate Bridge, civilians looked up asking the same question Wilson did a few months back: "Will we fit?"

A traditional Thanksgiving dinner was served, and afterwards, the sailors showed their families around the ship and their workspaces, hoping to reassure them that things would be fine while they were gone.

Phillip and Charlie stood on the flight deck in their winter coats, watching the Navy planes put on a show off the port side of the ship. There were high-speed fly-bys, rolls, and steep climbs to demonstrate the efficiency of the planes and their pilots. Charlie jumped when one of the fighters flew by, dropping ordnance in the water.

Phillip put his arm around her, reassuring her it was just noise, maybe a little louder than she was used to on the Fourth of July. They got back to Alameda just before sunset, ending the perfect day.

Phillip gave Charlie a hug, explaining that he had a duty and had to stay aboard. As he watched them walking away, he was glad that Renee had brought her car back to school so they didn't have to take the bus. He had told them not to stop in Oakland on their way back, as it wasn't that friendly of a city at night.

Chapter 19 : Underway

Christmas was nearing, so the crew had put up a small tree and a few decorations to make it more like home for those who wouldn't be with their families this year. The USS Midway wasn't much for holiday cheer—all metal surfaces and cramped quarters—but someone had strung twinkling lights along the mess hall ceiling. A plastic Santa with a sunburn (someone's idea of a joke) stood watch as you entered for chow. Phillip sent home a Christmas card with the ship on it, explaining that he wouldn't be joining them this year.

"You're really not going back?" Charlie asked, leaning against the door frame of her dorm room, with a hint of concern in her eyes. "Your mom's going to be heartbroken."

Phillip sighed, "I called her last week. She understands." He didn't mention the slight catch in his mother's voice, or how she'd quickly changed the subject to ask about the weather in San Francisco.

Charlie was going back to Hawaii for the winter break to be with her family. She had described Christmas in Kauai with such vivid detail that Phillip could almost feel the warm breeze and the tropical winds blowing in from the Pacific.

"Well, if you change your mind, there's always room for one more," she offered, though they both knew he wouldn't.

The day at the airport gate, Phillip caught Charlie's eye as she boarded her plane. Soon, she would be flying over the vast Pacific to her family's warm embrace. He would drive down the coast with his shipmates who, like him, had chosen to create their own holiday tradition rather than revisit the past.

That afternoon, they started the drive down the Pacific Coast Highway. Carlos took the wheel first, with Wilson riding shotgun and Johansen sprawled across the back seat next to Phillip.

The rental car—a convertible that Johansen had somehow talked the agency into upgrading them to—hugged the curves of the coastal road as they headed south.

"Trust me," Johansen said, his Minnesota accent thickening with excitement. "Christmas in Southern California beats freezing our asses off back home. We'll hit Pismo Beach, Avila Beach, and Santa Barbara on our way down."

Carlos glanced in the rearview mirror; sunglasses perched on his nose despite the winter clouds. "So, you guys have never been to Disneyland?" He shook his head in mock disappointment. "Man, you haven't lived."

They spent that night in a motel in San Luis Obispo, sharing two rooms between the four of them. Johansen snored loudly enough that Phillip found himself staring at the ceiling, thinking about his father and the Christmas traditions they wouldn't share this year.

On Christmas Day, the car pulled into a somewhat empty parking lot.

"We're here," Carlos announced with the pride of a local showing off his hometown. Disneyland—a place where Phillip's father was once offered a job as a cartoonist after the war. His father had turned down the opportunity, stating drawing was a hobby and not a job.

"Sometimes I wonder what would have happened if I'd taken that job," he had confessed to Phillip on his fifteenth birthday, showing him sketches he'd kept all these years.

The park was surprisingly busy despite the holiday, families in matching sweaters and Santa hats rushing from ride to ride. Phillip found himself enjoying the childlike wonder of it all—the parades, the music, even the overpriced food. As they watched the fireworks that night, he felt a peculiar peace settle over him. Perhaps this was exactly where he needed to be.

They headed back North after they left Disneyland, stopping on a beach outside of Los Angeles. They built a bonfire and toasted with Boone's Farm wine, while eating San Francisco sourdough bread and hard sausage before sprawling out on the beach for the evening.

After the holidays, everything was about getting ready to deploy. The easy camaraderie of their road trip carried back to the ship, where they found themselves preparing for the months ahead. It would be an adventure that was both exciting and terrifying to the shellbacks making their first voyage. The seasoned sailors like Manu tried to prepare the newer ones, but some experiences couldn't be explained, only lived through.

The night before they were scheduled to depart, Phillip couldn't sleep. He slipped out of his bunk and made his way to the flight deck, where the San Francisco Bay stretched before him, the city lights reflecting on the dark water. The Bay Bridge stood in a silhouette against the night sky, promising adventure on the other side.

Charlie and Renee made the drive to see the boys off.

She talked about the difficulty of getting on the post because out front was a large gathering of protesters, slowing everything down. Charlie asked Phillip about Disneyland.

"It was..." Phillip searched for the right word. "It was exactly what I needed."

Phillip got all the details about Hawaii and couldn't wait to get there to see for himself, since it would be the ship's first stop.

The whistle blew, signaling it was time for all sailors to come aboard. Kisses and hugs that were a little longer and a little tighter were given to those they would be leaving behind. As they went back aboard, you could see the smoke rising from the stack as signal flags fluttered in the morning breeze.

The fog was lifting, giving way to a bright, cold, sunny day. The USS Midway sailed with the morning tide, as the Navy Band played "Anchors Aweigh." You could see families frantically waving goodbye as they tried to find their sailor waving back from the flight deck. The sailors hurried below to change out of their dress blues and put on their work attire.

Most of the sailors who didn't have any responsibilities

for getting the ship to open water came back to the flight deck. Talking, watching, and taking photos as they approached the Golden Gate Bridge. The last resemblance of home they would see for the next ten months.

Charlie, Renee, and a few of her college friends were standing on the bridge holding the biggest flag Phillip had ever seen. The girls were waving, and all the sailors were waving back.

Phillip softly said to himself, "See you in ten months," a message to Charlie as well as to a city he had come to love.

They entered the open water, and the hills of the city grew more distant. They mentally prepared themselves for whatever waited on the horizon. And Phillip, for the first time in months, found himself looking forward to the journey.

As they got closer to San Diego, the ship began to come alive as flight deck crews went to their stations in preparation to land the flight group that would be carrying out the air operations once they got into the Tonkin Gulf. The thunder of the ship's engines mixed with the shouts of sailors calling to one another across the deck, their voices nearly lost in the Pacific breeze.

1st Class Petty Officer Ron Franklin was in a flight suit and aboard the rescue helicopter hovering on the starboard side, just in case there was a sea rescue needed.

Phillip, 2nd Class Manu, and Johansen, wearing their white jerseys, were under the island, meeting the requirements of having three corpsmen on deck, looking out at the well-choreographed display of men and machines going about their duties. The deck crew in their colored jerseys—yellow for aircraft directors, green for catapult and arresting gear crews, blue for aircraft handlers—moved with practiced efficiency across the non-skid surface.

Headsets were tested between the deck boss, the LSO (Landing Signal Officer), and the air boss. Phillip listened intently as orders came over their system while watching sailors carry out those orders with precision.

They were just a little over two miles out from San Diego, the distance that allows for a safe and efficient recovery process, as well as ensuring the carrier was in a position to support the flight group as the air wing came aboard.

The coastline of Southern California was visible in the distance, promising a brief respite before their arrival in Hawaii at Pearl Harbor.

One by one, each plane came in, announcing its approach with a deafening roar as the LSO guided them to the deck, "quarter mile, call the ball."

The deck vibrated beneath their feet with each arrested landing, the tailhook grabbing the cable with a violent jerk that never failed to impress Phillip. Once aboard, they were immediately detached from the cable by a deckhand and attached to a tractor that pulled the plane over to the elevator to be taken below, as the wings were either folded up or back.

The orchestrated movement reminded Phillip of a complex dance, using multi-million-dollar aircraft as their partners.

By the end of the operation, Air Wing Five was aboard. The air wing included squadrons like VF-161 (Chargers, F-4B), VF-151 (Vigilantes, F-4B), VA-93 (Blue Blazers, A-7B), VA-56 (Champions, A-7B), VA-115 (Arabs, A-6A & KA-6D), and VFP-63 Det 3 (Eyes of the Fleet, RF-8G). These were the pilots and crews who would soon be flying missions over Vietnam. This reality hung silently in the minds of everyone aboard. 120 aircraft had now completed the ship's readiness.

"Flight quarters are secured. The smoking lamp is lit in

all designated areas," came the announcement over the ship's general announcing system. The tension on the flight deck immediately eased as the ship settled back into its normal sea activity. Phillip and Carlos found a corner where they could play cribbage, smoke, and drink endless cups of coffee until their shift ended at midnight.

When at sea, there were two shifts: midnight to noon or noon to midnight. It didn't matter which you had because below deck, you wouldn't know if the sun was up or down.

The fluorescent lights of the passageways and compartments created a timeless environment where only the ship's bells marking the hours and the change of watches gave any indication of the passing day.

Sometimes Phillip would lose track of whether he'd been awake for four hours or fourteen, the monotonous hum of machinery and recycled air becoming the only constant in his world. For now, though, with Hawaii approaching and the successful recovery of the air wing complete, there was a sense of accomplishment that permeated the carrier, from the captain on the bridge to the most junior seaman in the depths of the engine room.

After a week of sliding through the Pacific, watching dolphins playfully swimming alongside them in water so blue and clear you could almost imagine seeing the bottom, the sailors went about carrying out the daily activities on the ship. The ocean stretched endlessly in all directions; a vast expanse of deep azure that made the massive carrier seem small by comparison.

Men like Phillip, Carlos, Wilson, and Johansen, who had grown up in landlocked states, stood transfixed at the rails during their breaks, listening to the sounds of the water as the ship cut through it.

The PA system came to life, as the captain's voice resonated through every compartment: "Attention all hands. We will be arriving at Pearl Harbor at 1000 hours. All ship's crew who are not essential to the ship's movement are ordered below to change into their dress whites for the ceremonial salute to the USS Arizona when we come alongside, that is all."

In the berthing compartments, men carefully put on their whites, ensuring every crease was perfect, every button polished to a high shine. This wasn't just another uniform inspection—this was a show of respect to fallen brothers they had never met but with whom they shared an unbreakable bond.

Upon reaching the entrance to Pearl Harbor, sailors

from enlisted to officers stood shoulder to shoulder around the ship's perimeter, looking out at the hallowed waters. The morning sun cast a golden glow across the harbor, highlighting the memorial's stark white structure against the blue backdrop of the Hawaiian sky. As the massive carrier slowed to a crawl, the only sounds were the gentle lapping of waves against the hull and the distant cry of seabirds.

As the ship came alongside the Memorial, the boatswain's whistle pierced the air, followed by the command: "Attention on deck! Hand salute!"

Five thousand arms rose in unison, five thousand pairs of eyes fixed straight ahead. The ship lowered the flag flying from the mast to half-staff, a timeless gesture of respect to the 1,177 sailors and Marines lost aboard the Arizona on that fateful December morning in 1941. The oil slick, referred to by many as "the tears of the Arizona," still rose from the sunken battleship, creating rainbow patterns on the water's surface more than three decades later.

They stood frozen at attention, the Hawaiian breeze gently rippling their white uniforms, until the ship had passed completely by the memorial and the flag was solemnly raised back to the top of the mast. Many of the men remained at the rails long after the order to stand down, just looking out.

Phillip would learn a few years later, after he got home from his service, that while he was casting his eye on the memorial, his first cousin, the oldest son of Art, and his wife were looking at him. Jim was on R and R from Vietnam for a week and had no idea his cousin was on the Midway, but he had a photo of that moment he would share later.

As Pearl Harbor opened up before them, with its bustling naval base and the lush green mountains of Oahu in the distance, the mood aboard the ship gradually lightened. Liberty awaited those fortunate enough to have shore leave.

Phillip had a 24-hour pass and, upon the announcement of liberty call, walked down the gangway to discover something Charlie already knew. It was paradise, a place where trade winds blew your troubles away and made palm branches move to the sounds of the island's music.

The water was blue, turquoise, combining as a white wave when it gently came ashore. The warm sun changed whatever mood you were in to one of tranquility and peace. The fragrance of the flowers was like being in an expensive candy store, and the colors were so vivid they couldn't be captured with a paintbrush.

Phillip spent his 24 hours soaking up everything he could. From the sands of Waikiki beach, the warmth of the sand and the water on his feet, to the people who moved around, not in a hurry, they were just happy to be there, and nothing could change that. Walking through the international trade area, there were street vendors lined up just off the main street in downtown Oahu. If you needed a souvenir, you could find it there.

But it was the sunsets that took Phillip's breath away. Now he understood what Charlie was trying to describe, but struggled to find the words. How do you find words to describe what was in front of him? He watched a sun that went from yellow to orange as it slowly sank into the water, to a blue so brilliant, it hurt your eyes. And then like magic, it disappeared as if someone had gently turned off the softest of lights. But the afterglow lingered, a promise written in fading color across the darkening sky: I will return tomorrow.

The time went by fast, and after the ship had been refueled, stores replenished, needed medical supplies inventoried and put away, weapons and armaments stored, it was time to say Aloha.

Phillip and Carlos made their way up to the catwalk to watch the island disappear from their sight, but never from their memory.

That evening, Phillip wrote a letter to Charlie and his parents describing what he saw, the sights that he captured on film, and tried to use words to describe a place he knew full well couldn't be explained in words. He wrote Anna saying, "You and Dad have to come and see this place. Because then you will have an idea what heaven may look like."

He was shaken out of his thoughts when he heard the PA system announce to turn to and clean the ship forward and aft. As he walked towards the sick bay, picking up a mop, he said to Johansen, "I guess no matter where we go, there are going to be some things that never change."

Johansen laughed out loud. "Yep, there are some things that never change," he said, as he put a stripper pad on the buffer.

They headed out to the open sea, knowing that the next time they would see land would be Subic Bay in the Philippines, a journey taking a little longer than two weeks. The weather had been good so far, and Phillip remembered an old Irish sailor's blessing: "May the seas lie smooth before you. May a gentle breeze forever fill your sails. May sunshine warm your face, and kindness warm your soul.

And, until we meet again, May God bless you and keep you safe."

Phillip whispered to himself, "Amen!"

Chapter 20: A Thousand Miles from Anywhere

The ship reached the point of no return in the Pacific Ocean, known as Point Nemo. This location is the furthest spot from any landmass, making it the most remote place on Earth. It's about 1,670 miles from the nearest land and far enough out to sea that the ship cannot be reached, making it a somewhat eerie experience for sailors who are now totally isolated. The vast emptiness of the endless blue horizon stretched in every direction, reinforcing their complete detachment from civilization.

As the captain explained where they were and that there would be no mail coming aboard or leaving for the next three days, a silence fell over the crew. Wilson, with a nervous habit of cracking jokes in tense moments, finally broke the quiet. "Well, I hope there aren't any storms coming because I can't swim over 1,600 miles," he said, forcing a smile that seemed insincere and not genuine.

Phillip couldn't even imagine how far that was and responded with a laugh, "That would be like swimming from

Iowa to San Francisco. Hell, I had a hard time with 300 meters without getting sucked under."

"I did in basic," Wilson replied, laughing more genuinely as he thought about their isolation.

That evening, as the ship settled into the rhythmic lull of nighttime operations, a silence descended upon the vessel. The day's duties complete, Phillip, Carlos, and Wilson seized their rare moment of freedom, stripping the pillows from their bunks and quietly making their way through the corridors toward the flight deck.

The metal stairs clanged beneath their feet as they emerged into the open air, the vastness of the Pacific immediately enveloping them. The night watch officer nodded silently as they made their way to the observation net suspended alongside the deck, a web of sturdy ropes designed to catch anyone who might otherwise plummet into the ocean below.

As they eased themselves down, they lay back on their pillows and gazed upward. What greeted them made them breathless. With no light pollution for over a thousand miles in any direction, and the ship's exterior illumination dimmed to operational minimums, the night sky revealed itself in its fullest glory.

"Jesus," whispered Phillip. The word escaped his lips as reverence rather than profanity.

The sky above them wasn't the navy blue of coastal skies but an inky, velvet blackness pierced by millions—perhaps billions—of lights.

The stars didn't merely twinkle; they burned with fierce intensity, some brilliant white, others subtly red, or gold. The Milky Way wasn't just a faint smudge visible from shore, but a magnificent, shimmering river of stars that made its way across the heavens. Nebulae that would have been invisible anywhere else revealed themselves as delicate, colored clouds suspended in the darkness.

Carlos reached out as if he could touch the stars. His voice, usually boisterous, was hushed with awe. "I had a science teacher in high school who told us there were more stars in the universe than grains of sand on all the beaches on Earth. I thought she was nuts," he paused, "But now, I'm not so sure."

Wilson, usually quick with a joke, remained silent for a long moment before responding. "My grandfather told me stories about nights like this. I always thought he was exaggerating." He shook his head slowly. "He wasn't. If anything, he undersold it."

The three men fell silent again. In that moment, rank, age, background—none of it mattered.

They were simply three sailors sharing the profound privilege of witnessing something few people ever would. Time became meaningless as they drifted in and out of conversation, pointing out shooting stars and satellites, telling stories of childhood nights spent camping under much less impressive skies. Wilson, gazing deep into the vast expanse above, said, "There are a lot of souls going to hell tonight."

Phillip turned to him, "How's that?"

Wilson didn't shift his gaze from the heavens. "My mom said every time a star falls from the sky, someone has been condemned to hell."

"I don't believe that," Phillip said with a slight shake of his head.

"You don't believe in hell?" Wilson questioned, finally glancing over at his companion.

Phillip adjusted his arms under his pillow and sighed. "I don't know about that. But the God my pastor told me about and the unconditional love he has for us would never send one of his children to a place like that."

It was Phillip who finally noticed the first hints of dawn approaching, not from the East as one would expect, but an almost imperceptible fading of the stars as they surrendered to the coming day.

"We should head back," Phillip said.

The three men gathered their pillows, climbed carefully out of the net, and made their way back toward their quarters, where they would shower and start another day. They went about their business as if nothing extraordinary had happened. But something had changed. In their eyes now lived the memory of what true isolation offered, the unexpected gift of seeing the universe as it truly was, unfiltered and magnificent.

After reaching the flight deck, Phillip paused for a moment at the lightening sky. Tomorrow night, perhaps, they would come again. They had two more days at Point Nemo—two more nights under the most perfect stars any of them would ever see.

Flight operations started precisely at 0800. The flight deck buzzed with activity as many new, inexperienced pilots prepared to become more comfortable with the challenging task of taking off from and landing on the carrier.

One by one, pilots took their turns hooking up to the

catapult. When ready, they were shot forward with tremendous force as the catapult slammed, sending their aircraft airborne while a cloud of steam announced each departure.

One of the crucial lessons that new pilots had to learn was to release their hands from the controls before launch. The initial acceleration during a catapult shot could be so intense that it potentially led to incorrect pilot responses— trying to pull up or push down on the control stick could cause the aircraft to veer dangerously off course. Difficult as it was, they had to refrain from touching the stick until they became airborne.

After launching, many aircraft would initially experience a brief descent after leaving the ship's deck because they haven't yet reached sufficient speed to achieve proper lift. The relatively short flight deck on an aircraft carrier prevented planes from accelerating to the necessary speed before reaching the end of the deck, even with the use of their afterburners for thrust. Consequently, each plane would momentarily fall below its target altitude before the pilot pulled the stick, causing the aircraft to rise upward and regain stability.

Throughout the morning, pilots ran touch-and-goes and go-arounds, working on lining up their aircraft with the pitch and yaw of the carrier to achieve smooth landings. The ship turned into the wind, with waves slapping against the hull, pitching it in ways that made this practice critical for younger, less experienced pilots. They focused intently on adjusting speed, watching their instruments to ensure proper alignment, and catching the arresting cables with their landing hooks.

The noise was deafening on the flight deck despite the protective headgear worn by all personnel. The roar of jet engines mingled with the sharp snap of arresting wires catching landing hooks and the hiss of steam catapults launching aircraft back into the sky. Color-coded crew members scurried across the deck in a choreographed dance of controlled chaos.

Phillip felt the heat radiating from the non-slip flight deck that provided crucial traction on the wet, rocking surface. As the sun rose in the sky, the heat cut through his flight suit, causing sweat to run down his neck and occasionally into his eyes. He listened intently to the voices coming through his headset.

"Ghost Rider 207, you are on final approach, winds 15 knots, call the ball," came the voice in his headset.

"207, ball," Harrison responded, acknowledging visual

contact with the optical landing system.

He reduced power slightly, keeping his eyes locked on the amber "meatball." The illuminated ball's lights would guide his approach angle.

Below on the deck, the LSOs (Landing Signal Officers) watched his approach critically. "Wave off, you're too high, go around," the LSO instructed. The aircraft flew over the flight deck, climbing back in altitude to try again.

Later in the afternoon, after what had been a rather routine day on the flight deck, an A-4 Skyhawk was handed off by the marshal controller to the LSO.

"Diamondback 220, continue on glide path, maintain your speed." The LSO made his last observation and said, "Quarter mile, call the ball."

"Ball," answered the pilot as he guided his plane toward the deck.

"Bolter!" yelled the LSO, letting the pilot know he hadn't caught a wire. But to the surprise of everyone who heard the announcement, the pilot started slowing down instead of maintaining speed for the go-around.

"Bolter, bolter! Damn it, BOLTER!" the LSO shouted urgently as the plane started to drift over the angled deck.

For a heart-stopping moment, the aircraft disappeared from view over the edge of the deck.

Then came the thunderous boom of the afterburner engaging, and the plane reappeared, climbing steeply with seawater visibly dripping from its landing gear.

When the pilot finally came aboard after being cleared for another approach, he was immediately summoned to the Air Boss. The pilot knew what was coming—an intense dressing-down followed by being grounded for a few weeks. It was the worst punishment a naval aviator could face because to them, flying wasn't just a job—it was everything.

Down in sick bay, there were sailors getting attention for various lacerations, contusions, and the normal things you would see in your doctor's office. There were a few more serious injuries, like dislocated shoulders from hitting something that didn't want to give, falls, and feet that snapped when something was dropped on them. But there was one Marine who was running a low-grade fever and complaining of stomach pain. It wasn't isolated, but his white blood cell count showed that he had some sort of bacterial infection. An IV was started with an antibiotic to fight off the ailment, and he was kept for observation.

Later that evening, he seemed to get worse. After the

doctor did another examination, he discovered that the pain was isolated in the lower right quadrant of the Marine's abdomen.

"He has rebound tenderness," Johansen said. "Better go wake the surgeon."

The surgeon was summoned and, upon his examination, confirmed it was the patient's appendix and it needed to come out immediately.

"McManus, you still on duty?"

"Yes, sir," came his reply.

"Well, have you ever assisted on an appendectomy?"

"No, sir, but I know the procedure if you want me to scrub in."

"Yes, get the Marine prepped and scrub in. I'll get the anesthesiologist."

Now Phillip was hoping he hadn't spoken out of turn. He knew the procedure, but doing surgery on a ship that rocks you to sleep was a new challenge.

Once the patient was asleep, the surgeon asked McManus for a #10 blade scalpel and made an oblique angle incision 4 inches long. He handed off that blade as

Phillip snapped another clean #10 blade into the surgeon's awaiting palm. As the surgeon started cutting the peritoneum, Phillip started clamping off bleeders so the surgeon could see as he worked. The surgeon drained any infection from the abdominal cavity, rinsing it with a sterile saline solution as Phillip suctioned out the wound. Finally, the surgeon tied off the appendix with sutures, detached it from the cecum, and removed it from the body, placing it in a specimen container that Phillip held ready. The surgeon ran a check on the cecum and surrounding area to ensure there weren't any other issues. He tied off the bleeders, removing the clamps Phillip had put on. Phillip handed the surgeon a drain. They placed sutures to close the peritoneum around the tube, followed by closing the subcutaneous tissue and skin. The patient was then transferred to recovery.

"Nice job, McManus," the surgeon said. "I guess the report you got from A School was spot on. You do have good hands."

"Thank you, sir, and thank you for letting me assist you."

The surgeon looked at him and said, "Well, don't be surprised if I call on you again if I need a hand. I like someone who knows what they're doing without telling me how they would do it."

Phillip laughed and said, "No, sir, I learned to keep my thoughts to myself a long time ago."

It was 0100 hours, so Phillip said, "Good night, Commander." As he walked back to his rack, he knew he had way too much adrenaline running to go to sleep. So instead, he turned on a light over his rack and wrote a couple of letters describing his day—one to his parents and one to Charlie, who would get a kick out of it. He knew they couldn't go anywhere yet, but he had them ready when mail resumed.

One of the things a sailor loves to do is pull one over on a Marine. The bridge officer summoned a young Marine to stand watch. He handed him a pair of binoculars and told him to be on the lookout for a large buoy, which is a floating marker anchored to the seabed, used as a navigational aid, warning of hazards, or to mark a channel.

"Once you see it, let me know so we can have the mail brought out to the ship," the officer instructed.

There was no such marker, but the Marine would scan the waters for hours, searching across the horizon. The commander walked away, chuckling to himself, knowing that this Marine had just been fooled; there was no such buoy.

They were getting close to Subic Bay, and Phillip had

mail to read. One of the items he received was a carrot cake Charlie had made. He took it to sick bay to share with his shipmates over a morning cup of coffee. It was gone in minutes, despite the fact that with the mail handling, it was in pieces. He would keep that part to himself when he sent a letter thanking Charlie for the treat.

Chapter 21: From Shore to War

They pulled out, or maybe "kicked out" is a better description, of Subic Bay earlier than originally planned. The USS Midway's hasty departure left a wake of relief among many of the officers and resentment among most of the enlisted men who'd barely had time to spend their hard-earned pay. Subic Bay made Tijuana, Mexico, look like a 3-star resort. The Philippines' port was a feast for the senses—all of them assaulted at once. The stench hit you first: a pungent mixture of rotting tropical vegetation, open sewage, and street food frying in days-old oil. The heat soaked through your whites within minutes of stepping off the ship.

As you crossed over the bridge connecting the naval base to Olongapo City, down below were young kids swimming in a river the sailors called "shit river," a murky channel filled with waste and dirty water. Thin brown bodies glistened as they called up to passing sailors.

"Hey Joe! Throw me a coin!" they shouted, eager to dive and retrieve whatever small treasure they could grab before it hit bottom. Some sailors obliged, watching with amazement as children as young as five jumped into the filth for a few

American cents.

In town, there were bars and gift shops everywhere you looked, their neon signs flashing even in daylight. With names to appeal to homesick sailors—"Texas Bar," "California Girls," "New York, New York"—though none bore any resemblance to their namesakes.

Hawkers stood outside each entrance, grabbing at passing sleeves: "Hey sailor, you come in! Number one bar!"

The local girls lounged in doorways or at the bars, some barely out of their teens, who were willing to spend the night with you for a can of coffee or maybe a few American cigarettes—commodities worth far more than the few pesos they might otherwise earn in a week.

Inside the bars, Filipino bands played American rock hits with the reverb turned up to eleven, partly to energize the crowd but mostly to cover their accents as they worked through Beatles songs, Rolling Stones, and Creedence Clearwater Revival. And of course, the green, green grass of home by Tom Jones. The singers studied American records religiously, mimicking every inflexion as they played their worn-out instruments.

The beer was bad—barely cold—but it was cheap, and

after the third or fourth bottle, nobody much cared about the taste. Shore Patrol moved through the crowds in pairs, their white helmets and armbands visible warnings, keeping a watchful eye out for sailors who had too much to drink, falling asleep, or deciding that tonight was a good night to start a fight.

Veterans warned the new guys: "Keep one hand on your wallet and the other on your drink."

Phillip, along with Johansen and Carlos, had seen enough, so they decided to head back on base to the EM club. Bad idea. With the Midway in port along with the USS Oriskany, another carrier, as well as a troop ship full of Marines who had stopped before deploying to Vietnam, the club was beyond crowded. If you sat at the bar, you couldn't get away. If you were trying to get to the bar, you were out of luck.

With the heat, humidity, and a bunch of Marines in a bad mood, a fight soon broke out. Someone threw a punch, and the whole place erupted. Fists, tables, and chairs were flying everywhere. It took about 50 Shore Patrol and about 40 minutes before everyone was heading back to their ships.

The next morning, the USS Midway was heading back to sea to join the Enterprise, already stationed in the Tonkin

Gulf. The captain came over the PA system the next day, scolding the sailors' behavior and asking the question 'Why?\

Captain Carroll said, "Look, I understand these things happen. But we got kicked out of port because you were fighting with your own shipmates. Hell, look at their patch before you start throwing a punch."

Phillip, along with other corpsmen, was busy treating sailors who didn't fare so well in the scuffle. Cuts that needed closing, concussions requiring monitoring, busted-up knuckles, and sprains that had to be wrapped. In all, there were around 40 sailors who were on light duty and faced the possibility of a Captain's mast. Some were handed off to the Marine guard, after treatment, to be taken back to the brig.

In a few days, what had seemed like a fun night in Subic Bay, being entertained by the local women, brought over 100 of the ship's sailors into sick bay for treatment for STDs, particularly gonorrhea. The senior medical officer, Commander Richardson, sent out a strongly worded message to each department head, informing them of this alarming issue and their urgent need to communicate what options were available to those seeking entertainment with local women.

Commander Richardson wrote, "Effective immediately,

there will be condoms available at the gangway when your sailors go on liberty call. They need to take them or keep it in their pants. Any sailor reporting to sick bay from this point forward with an STD because they didn't follow orders given by a senior officer assigned to this ship will be referred to the JAG officer for disciplinary action."

Captain Carroll backed up the medical officer's directive with his own announcement over the ship's PA system later that afternoon. "What you do on your liberty is your business," he said, his voice tinged with frustration, "but when it affects this ship's readiness, I make it my business. We cannot afford to have our mission compromised because of poor judgment. The mission comes first, that is all."

A few junior officers, concerned about permanent marks on their service records, were quietly approaching senior staff about keeping these "indiscretions" confidential. Chief Medical Officer Richardson made it clear that from this point forward, proper protocol would be followed for every case, regardless of rank.

The ship arrived at Yankee Station, which was located about 100 miles offshore of South Vietnam, due east of Dong Hoi in the Tonkin Gulf, to start their mission. One that was considered critical to the war effort: disrupting supplies from

North Vietnam to the South, conducting aerial attacks against enemy installations, transportation routes, and lines of communication.

The USS Midway joined the other carriers already on station, a floating city of steel and firepower that never slept. From the air, they must have looked like distant gray specks on the South China Sea—insignificant until you witnessed what they could unleash.

As the sun was rising in the east, and the captain turned the ship onto the wind, Phillip and Almadova scanned the activities on the flight deck, looking for any signs of incidents that would require their attention. As corpsmen, they knew that on this floating acre of intense activities, injuries could happen in a heartbeat.

Each sailor was in his color-coded shirt, identifying who they were and what their job was on the deck. It also made it easy for the Air Boss, who was responsible for everything happening below his watchful eye.

Planes were brought up to the flight deck from the hangar below, armament carefully attached to their wings and fuselages. Each bomb, missile, and gun had to be precisely mounted—a mistake could mean disaster for everyone.

Phillip watched as ordnance crews in their red shirts moved with practiced precision, their hands working deftly despite the bulky gloves they wore. Once armed, the aircraft taxied over to the catapults, where they were secured for launch.

Phillip and Manu watched the blast deflector go up, and then the shooter giving the signal to the pilot—a salute before dropping down and pointing as the catapult launched the aircraft with an acceleration that would reach a speed of 170 mph in about 2 seconds and with forces that pushed the pilots back into their seats.

Plane after plane launched. And even though you wore headsets or ear protection, the sound pierced your ears as they were flung off the ship like a rock hurled from a slingshot. The catapults shook your body when they reached the end with a thud, only to be brought back, prepared for the next plane, and fired again. The deck crew moved with the precision of a Swiss watch.

Being turned into the wind—necessary for successful launches and recoveries—the sailors had a difficult time as they had to navigate remaining upright while carrying out their duties. They leaned into the wind, the gusts sometimes strong enough to blow tools or unsecured equipment clear off the deck and into the waters below.

When the operation was over, the order came to "stand down." Nothing to do but wait for those birds to come back to their nest. The sudden quiet felt almost unnatural after the controlled mayhem of launch.

Phillip walked the deck during these lulls, looking for debris that might become a potential hazard. He'd stood at the edge of the deck, imagining the havoc that was going to be released by the planes that had just departed. Soon, they would be dropping their payloads on jungle supply routes, bridges, or ammunition dumps.

"Hey McManus!" someone yelled, and as Phillip turned around, he saw Johansen helping a sailor who had been injured. The man was cradling his right hand, pain evident on his face.

"I'm taking him below to get his hand looked at. Do you want to get a cup of coffee before they come home?" Johansen asked.

"Sounds like a plan," Phillip replied, giving a thumbs up.

They walked the sailor down to sick bay, and the X-ray showed he had a broken hand. The accident occurred while he was trying to secure a 500-pound bomb to the wing of an

A-6 Intruder. The bomb had shifted unexpectedly, catching his hand between it and the mounting bracket.

"Nothing serious," the doctor said, looking at Wilson and telling him to put a plastic cast on it up to his elbow. The sailor looked relieved, not so much about the diagnosis but because it meant he wouldn't be sent off the carrier.

As they relaxed with a much-needed cigarette and a cup of coffee that had been sitting on the stove too long, Phillip thought about the controlled chaos that would take place when it was time to recover the aircraft and hoped all of them would make it back safely.

Phillip's day was done, so he went up to the bridge area to watch the recovery. He knew he wasn't going to get any sleep until operations for the day were completed. He actually liked the recovery better than the launch. It was less hectic because there were fewer people on the deck, and there was no ordnance to worry about. From his vantage point, he could see the entire flight deck illuminated against the darkening sky. The horizon was a thin line between deep blue water and the dusk settling in. The deck was cleared except for the yellow-shirted landing signal officers and the necessary crash crews standing by. Blue-shirted aircraft handlers waited with their chains, ready to secure each aircraft the moment it touched down.

Through his headset, he could hear each pilot making adjustments to their approach as the air traffic controllers got them closer to the ship. The controlled, professional voices belied the tension of what was about to happen.

"November Foxtrot, what is your fuel state?" a controller asked, his voice calm but insistent.

"One point three," came the response from the pilot, meaning he had 1,300 pounds of fuel remaining—enough for another attempt if he missed the wire, but not much beyond that.

The cable was adjusted for the weight of the plane and pilot or pilots to assure a safe landing. Each aircraft had its own optimal setting—a miscalculation could mean a broken cable, a damaged aircraft, or worse.

One by one, the planes came aboard, each approach ending in a controlled crash as the aircraft slammed onto the deck. The arresting gear groaned under the strain, cables stretching and then gradually stopping each plane from hurtling into the ocean beyond. Some missed the arresting gear and would have to go around and try again, the pilots applying full throttle even as their wheels touched down, with the LSO saying "bolter."

Phillip watched the recovery operation. The rhythm was broken when an F-4B Phantom notified CATCC, Carrier Air Traffic Control Center, that they had an AIM-9 Sidewinder still attached to his wing that he couldn't shake loose.

Normally, if a plane still had ordnance it hadn't disposed of because of cloud cover or other factors, they would go to a designated free-drop zone and dispose of it before returning to the carrier.

The primary reason for this protocol was the added weight and resulting stress on the wings, landing gear, and weapons pylons during landing. Additionally, the risk of accidental detonation of the ordnance was a concern, as bombs are usually armed just before release. But sometimes, as in this case, the ordnance simply wouldn't release.

The pilot was told to go back to marshal—the holding patterns several miles from the carrier—and that he would be the last plane recovered.

As he approached the carrier for his first attempt, he dumped fuel, leaving enough for landing twice if needed. Phillip knew this was standard procedure: lighten the aircraft as much as possible without sacrificing safety margins.

The deck was cleared of all non-essential personnel, and the crash crews tensed, ready for any eventuality. Over the radio, Phillip heard the Landing Signal Officer say, "Quarter mile, call the ball." The "ball" was the optical landing system—a yellow light that guided pilots to the correct glide path.

"Ball," called the pilot, his voice steady despite what had to be extraordinary pressure.

Everyone turned to watch as the F-4 came in, its approach looking textbook perfect. Nose up, hook down, and as he caught the wire, the nose came down hard and the Sidewinder missile slid across the angled deck, falling harmlessly into the sea below. There was a collective exhale from everyone watching.

The next sound was the Air Boss congratulating everyone with his well-known words of appraisal: "Shit hot!" The phrase, delivered in his gravelly voice over the loudspeaker, was more coveted than any formal commendation.

Operations were now concluded. The ship changed course to steam downwind, and everyone was back aboard, safe and waiting to do it all again tomorrow. The deck crews swarmed over the aircraft, getting them below to the hangar deck and securing them.

As Phillip came up to the flight deck, now lit only by the full moon that cast elongated shadows across the ship, he looked over to the catapults where two F-14 Tomcats sat ready to be launched at a moment's notice. Their sleek, predatory silhouettes were unmistakable even in the dim light. The pilots sat idle in the cockpit, awaiting orders to go but hoping they wouldn't come.

The night air was cooler now, carrying the mingled scents of jet fuel, salt spray, and hot metal. Phillip took a deep breath, savoring the relative quiet after a day filled with the unrelenting roar of engines. Out here, hundreds of miles from land, under a canopy of stars undimmed by city lights, it was easy to forget that somewhere beyond the horizon, a war was raging. But the ready fighters and their waiting pilots were a stark reminder of why they were all here.

The next morning, before flight operations were to begin, an E-2 Hawkeye was getting ready to head into port to deliver and pick up mail. But a sailor walked straight into the propeller. He took most of the impact to his head and face, the sound of the impact silencing the busy flight deck for a split second before chaos erupted.

"Corpsman!" someone yelled, their voice cracking with panic.

Manu and Phillip came running to the accident, medical bags clutched tightly in their hands, but they came to a halt when they saw the gruesome scene. There wasn't anything for them to do. The sailor was almost unrecognizable from the catastrophic injuries to his head and face. With practiced movements, Almadova removed the sailor's dog tags and placed the notch between his teeth, clamping the jaw down for identification. The sailor's body was solemnly placed in a body bag and sent below decks.

"What the hell was he thinking?" one sailor whispered, his face pale beneath his tan.

Phillip looked at him, eyes hollow from what they'd witnessed. "I guess we'll never know that answer."

Was it intentional or an accident? Was his mind on something else? Maybe thinking about home? Questions only he and God could now answer.

Later that day, his body was placed in a weighted canvas shroud, meticulously sealed according to naval tradition. A religious service was conducted by a Navy Chaplain on the flight deck, the drone of aircraft temporarily silenced out of respect. Sailors in their crisp dress whites stood at attention as six of the fallen man's shipmates lifted the shrouded body and, with ceremonial precision, lowered it over the side of the ship into the vast, indifferent ocean.

The captain would later notify the family of the date, time, and details about the accident. He would provide them with the exact coordinates where their son's body was committed to the sea, along with the folded flag that had said goodbye to him—a triangle of stars and stripes that would never fill the void left behind.

Chapter 22: Monkey Mountain

On April 30th, the Midway had completed its first 90 days of operations and was being replaced by the USS Oriskany for a much-needed break. As the ship departed back to Subic Bay, the flight surgeon, along with Chief Mitchell, called Phillip and Carlos into his office.

"I have a special mission for one of you," the flight surgeon began, leaning back in his chair. "We have been asked to send a Corpsman into Da Nang for a short period of time. You will be attached to an aid station at Monkey Mountain at the Da Nang Air Base, working with the 2nd Battalion, 1st Marines. You will stay with them until a suitable replacement can be sent from the States." He looked between the two young men. "Who wants the assignment?"

Phillip and Martinez looked at each other and both raised their hands. The competition between them was friendly but real—the chance to put their training to use was exciting.

The chief sighed. "I need one. You two work it out and let me know by the end of the day." He dismissed them with a wave of his hand.

After a discussion followed by a coin flip, Phillip approached the Chief later that afternoon. The Chief looked up from his paperwork with a knowing smile.

"So, McManus, I take it you won the flip?"

"Yes, sir," answered Phillip, trying to keep the excitement from his voice. This would be his first time on Vietnamese soil, and despite the dangers, he couldn't help feeling a thrill of anticipation.

"Okay. You will be leaving the ship on the C-123 Provider tomorrow when it goes in to get the mail. Everything you will need will be provided when you arrive. Here are your orders." The Chief handed over a manila envelope with official papers inside.

Phillip looked at the orders and, seeing his name already typed on them, scratched his head as he read them. "How in the hell did they know it would be me?" he muttered.

The Chief just smiled. "Let's just say I've worked with you two long enough to know how a coin flip between you and Martinez would turn out."

That evening, Phillip packed a few personal items and

made sure he had stationery from the Midway so his parents or Charlie wouldn't worry, or even know he had left the ship. He would date his letters from the carrier as if nothing had changed. No sense causing unnecessary concern back home with news of his temporary reassignment to a combat zone.

The next morning, Phillip boarded the plane for the short ride into Da Nang. From the sky, everything looked peaceful. The landscape was a patchwork of emerald rice paddies, lush vegetation, and scattered villages with thatched roofs reflecting the morning sun.

As they got closer, Phillip pressed his face against the window and saw the Air Base come into view. It stood in stark contrast to the natural beauty he first saw—a place dominated by military infrastructure cut into the countryside. The base was a bustling hub of activity, with numerous aircraft parked on the runways and taxiways, alongside rows of tents and prefabricated structures for housing and operations.

The controller's voice crackled over the headset. "We are temporarily holding you from landing. The Vietnamese have launched a mortar attack on the base perimeter."

Phillip could see a platoon of Marines deploying from the

283

southern edge of the base, into the jungle to push back the attackers—a unit Phillip would join soon.

A few minutes later, they were cleared for landing. The wheels touched down with a jolt on the pockmarked runway.

After deplaning, he walked briskly to the headquarters building, his bag slung over one shoulder, sweat already soaking through his uniform in the humid air. He presented his orders to a corporal who barely glanced up from his paperwork.

"Another Navy corpsman? I will show you to your quarters."

The young corporal motioned for Phillip to follow. They walked in silence past a row of sandbagged bunkers and communication towers until they reached a cluster of tents set back from the main compound.

"Home sweet home, Doc," the corporal said, holding open the tent flap. "Uniforms are laid out on your rack, along with the Marine Corps manual for corpsmen. You'll want to read that front to back. The guys will be counting on you."

Phillip nodded, taking in the sparse accommodations. A single cot with a thin mattress, a footlocker at its end, and mosquito netting draped from above.

"I'll tell the Gunny you're here," the corporal said, already backing toward the tent entrance.

Phillip sat down on the edge of his rack and ran his hands over his face, wiping the sweat from his eyes. This wasn't the sterile hospital environment he'd trained in. This was Vietnam. He reached for the Marine Corps manual and began to read. Whatever came next, he needed to be ready.

As Phillip sat reading, he heard a series of pop, pop, pops. Looking out of his tent, he saw a Marine sitting on a crate shooting at something. As he was looking, a voice said, "Rats, the damn things are as big as cats back home." Phillip turned to see a very large man standing in his tent. He had to be 6'4" and 240 pounds, his rolled-up sleeves exposing biceps as big as his calves.

"Name's Gunnery Sergeant Miller. Been here nine months. Don't worry, kid. You'll get your bearings. First week's the hardest," he said, extending a calloused hand.

"Okay, follow me," the man said. "I'm going to show you around and cover some items you need to know, so try to keep up. Over there is the aid station, where the docs are caring for servicemen as well as area civilians who are being affected by this war and suffering from Typhoid Fever, Tuberculosis, and rabies from these damn rats. There's the mess hall, and that's the zoo. Place to get a beer but gets a little rowdy at times."

As they walked between the structures, the humid air clung to Phillip's skin like a second uniform. The scent of diesel fuel, medicinal alcohol, and something distinctly foreign filled his nostrils. In the distance, helicopters circled like mechanical dragonflies.

"Med school teach you about treating jungle rot?" Miller asked with a knowing smile. "Didn't think so. You'll be an expert so."

He went on saying, "As you probably saw earlier, we get harassed by small units on the perimeter. These guerrilla fighters probe our defenses under the cover of the jungle, testing our response times, and it's our job to move these units away from our base and establish a buffer zone.

However, most of the time they're gone by the time we get out there—nothing but footprints and empty shell casings left behind. But once in a while, we make contact with them, and when that happens, Charlie pays the price." He paused, his weathered face hardening as he gazed across the clearing toward the tree line. "Last week, our patrol cornered a squad of them trying to set up a mortar position. Didn't end well for them. That's the game out here—cat and mouse until someone gets caught in the open."

Each day was the same. The night before patrol, Philip would inventory his med bag to make sure he had all essential tools for field treatment, including dressings, bandages, morphine, IV supplies, and instruments for minor surgery. Stethoscope, otoscope, and a Minor Surgery Kit with scissors, clamps, scalpels, and tweezers for minor procedures he could use in the field. And of course, sutures and sterilized silk for closing wounds.

"Everything is here," he murmured as he closed the bag. Then he would try to get some sleep. But between the heat, mosquitoes that the net didn't keep out, and the buzz of an active airbase, sleep was something he would need to catch up on when he was back aboard his ship.

The skies were still dark as the platoon gathered and moved out a few yards. There, they would sit quietly, waiting for the sun to awaken to another day. Some grabbed a smoke, while others checked their equipment or stole a few more minutes of sleep. The smell of the jungle crept into your nose as you sat quietly, earthy, damp, and somehow both alive and decaying at the same time.

The Gunnery Sergeant asked Phillip if he had his M1911A1 pistol. Phillip said yes, finding it strange his job was to treat wounds, not make them.

The Gunny saw the question in Phillip's eyes and said, "Here, they don't play by the rules. That red cross and no weapon makes you a prime target."

"Move out," came the command. They would go out on their perimeter about 2 clicks, just over a mile, searching for VC. Half hoping to make contact, and the other half hoping it was just a long walk in the jungle.

Philip adjusted the weight of his med bag across his shoulders. Unlike the others, his burden was double—both the standard gear and his medical supplies. The platoon called him "Doc," though he was only a corpsman, not a physician. But to them, he was the closest thing to a doctor they had right now.

As they moved through the thick vegetation, Sergeant Ferguson fell in beside him. "How'd you sleep, Doc?" he asked, his voice barely above a whisper.

"About as well as you'd expect," Philip replied.

They continued in silence for the next hour, the humid air already causing sweat to soak through their fatigues despite the early hour.

The Lieutenant held up his fist, signaling a halt. The platoon froze in place, each man scanning their sector. Philip's heart rate quickened.

"Listen up," the Gunny said softly as the squad leaders gathered around him. "Intelligence reports increased activity in this sector. Stay alert!"

As they moved forward again, Phillip went over mental checklists of treatments—what to do for gunshot wounds, shrapnel, burns, shock. He had seen a photo of each, but never the actual wound he was thinking about. Hoping that when he did, he could focus on the wound, not the soldier, so he wouldn't throw up.

Charlie had been probing the defenses under the cover of darkness, testing response times and looking for cracks in them. And most of the time, they're gone by the time they get out there.

The jungle thickened as they moved deeper into their patrol route. Philip's senses were heightened, alert to any sound or movement that seemed out of place.

The sun was climbing higher now, burning away the morning mist and turning the jungle into a steam bath. Every breath felt thick with moisture, and the weight of the med bag seemed to double with each passing hour.

"We've got signs of recent activity," the Gunny informed them quietly. "Fresh tracks heading north. Stay alert, Doc, stay by my side."

Just then, they drew fire, coming from about 100 meters in front of them. The Marines spread out and started returning fire. Rounds and tracer fire marked the target. Ahead of Phillip, there was an explosion from a grenade. "I'm hit!" came the call.

Phillip, without thinking, grabbed his bag and started running toward the Marine.

"Doc's up," the Gunny shouted, and every weapon opened up to protect his movement. Phillip was running and zigzagging as fast as he could, but everything seemed to be in slow motion in his mind. The sounds overhead sounded like the biggest Fourth of July fireworks he had ever heard, but it felt like he was in the middle of it.

Phillip leaped to the ground, crawling the few feet to the wounded Marine with his med bag behind him. The other Marines were assaulting the VC, driving them deep into the jungle or, more likely, to their underground caves where they would stay until the cover of darkness.

"How is he?" the lieutenant asked.

Phillip didn't respond as he was too busy identifying the wounds and grabbing things from his bag.

"Open abdomen wound with his intestines exposed," he finally responded.

Phillip gave the Marine, who was in a great deal of pain, a shot of morphine and put the needle in his shirt collar, as he had been taught. He cut away clothing, being careful not to pull out anything that was embedded in the wound. He was able to stop most of the bleeding and was taking out a 12x12 sterile pad to cover the wound.

"Don't you need to put that back in?" asked the lieutenant.

"No, I don't know how much damage he has or if there might be shrapnel that could cause more harm if I did." Phillip's words were heard by the lieutenant, but were more for himself as he was going through each step. After loosely putting the large bandage over the wound, he opened a bag of sterile IV solution and soaked the bandage.

"I got to keep it wet," he said.

The sound of a helicopter could be heard, so they

moved the wounded Marine to the evac site and waited. Phillip immediately started an IV and opened it completely to get fluids in him, as he had lost a great deal of blood and it needed to be replaced with something. He took his blood pressure and gave him another shot of morphine. Again, he stuck the needle in his collar so the doctors and nurses back at the aid station would know how much he had been given.

They loaded the Huey, and it quickly took off, the door gunner firing just in case the VC wanted to show their heads.

"Doc, am I going to make it?" the wounded Marine asked.

Phillip looked into his face and, with a voice he hoped was more convincing than his eyes, said, "You got this. I have seen worse."

It was a lie, but he didn't want to tell him the truth, which was that he didn't know.

As Phillip monitored his vitals and kept the dressing wet, he couldn't help but look at this kid, probably 20, the same age as himself. He had so much in front of him if he could just hold on. Phillip was hoping he had done enough.

Once down, they were met by a surgical team who took him off the chopper and rushed him through the doors. His last words to Phillip were something about his mom. But with the noise from the chopper, he couldn't be exactly sure what it was. The only word he heard for sure was him asking about his mom.

The Gunny came over to Phillip, bumping him on the side, and said, "You were great out there today, Doc. Now go hit the shower."

Phillip threw his med bag on his bunk, grabbed his shaving pack and a towel, and headed to the shower. He was covered in blood, and it took a while to get it off and out from under his fingernails.

As he put on a clean uniform, he was already starting to sweat as if he hadn't toweled off at all. He walked over to get some chow before he checked on the young Marine. He walked through the door, scanned the beds, and asked one of the nurses if he could see the young Marine they brought in about an hour ago. She turned to look at Phillip and said, in a voice that had seen too much, "He didn't make it."

Phillip didn't say anything as he nodded his head and walked out the door. Slowly making his way to the zoo to get a beer, he felt his eyes swell up as a tear ran down his cheek. He wiped it away, recalling what the doctor told them in A School, "There are two rules you must never forget as a corpsman; Rule 1, in war, young men die, and Rule 2, no matter your training or skill, you can't change Rule 1."

Phillip walked over to the bar stool and ordered a beer. He went to grab some script out of his pocket, and the bartender said, "You're drinking free tonight."

Phillip looked around and saw a table of Marines raise their glass in his direction. He gave them a tip of his hat as he turned around and said, "Keep them coming until I feel numb."

Each day was the same, looking for someone who used the terrain to their advantage and never stayed around too long to fight it out. On what was to be Phillip's last night, the Gunny Sergeant came over to his tent and asked if he could come in.

"You're not going out with us tomorrow," he said.

Phillip put down the letter he was writing and asked why.

"Your replacement is here, and you're heading back to your ship," the Gunny replied.

Phillip felt relief as well as a little confusion. "Is he good to go for tomorrow?" Phillip asked.

"This isn't his first rodeo. He's ready." The Gunny went

on to explain that in the morning, he was to turn in his med bag back to the aid station, change into the flight suit he held in his hand, and take the uniforms back to HQ.

"Your orders are already cut."

Phillip asked the Gunnery Sergeant Miller, "Why the flight suit?"

"Not sure, but apparently you're going back to your ship by something other than what brought you."

They both stood up. The Gunny extended his hand and said, "If you ever get bored on that boat, you know you can come back here."

Phillip laughed, noticing he couldn't even see his hand in the Guney's big bear claw, and said, "No, I think the ship will be just fine. But take care, and thanks for looking after me."

"Anytime, Doc, anytime." He turned and ducked his head as he walked out of the tent.

Phillip went back to finishing his letter, deciding he would wait and mail it once he got back aboard his ship. He didn't have much to pack, so Phillip finished his letter, went over to eat, and then to the Zoo for a few beers. It might be a while before he got another chance to wet his whistle.

Chapter 23: Fuji-San and Golden Arches

After a hurried breakfast, Phillip trudged back to his tent through the busy compound. The morning air was already thick with humidity, promising another sweltering day. He gathered everything he had to turn in and made a final glance around the canvas shelter that used to be his home.

The aid station was a flurry of controlled chaos—nurses and medics rushing between patients. Things were too hectic for long goodbyes, handshakes, hugs, and short messages wishing him well.

After changing into his flight suit, Phillip headed over to the flight terminal. The olive drab fabric felt both foreign and familiar after weeks in combat fatigues. As he walked across the base, he took mental snapshots of the place he was leaving behind: helicopter mechanics hunched over exposed engines, a supply sergeant arguing with a clipboard-wielding officer, and fresh-faced replacements looking simultaneously eager and terrified. The everyday routine of an operating base at war continued, indifferent to his departure.

The flight terminal was little more than a corrugated metal building with a few plastic chairs and a battered operations desk. Phillip dropped his bag and sank into one of the chairs. The tropical heat and beads of sweat formed at his temples despite the relative shelter.

"We've got a McDonnell F-4 Phantom inbound to pick you up," the operations sergeant informed him, not looking up from his clipboard. "ETA forty minutes. It's heading back to your carrier." He paused, then added, "Apparently, there's an issue with one of the catapults, and it is heading to Yokosuka Naval Base in Japan to have it fixed. You're hitching a ride."

Phillip nodded, settling in for the wait. His thoughts drifted between memories of the past month—the missions, the close calls, the comrades—and apprehension about the high-speed flight ahead. The distant thunder of jet engines gradually grew louder. Through the smudged windows, Phillip saw the fighter jet taxiing over to the terminal. The canopy opened to reveal a helmeted figure inside. Moments later, a young Lieutenant with close-cropped blond hair and a confident stride approached the terminal. His flight suit bore the patches of VF-114, the "Aardvarks" squadron.

Phillip stood at attention and offered a crisp salute as the officer reached him. Lieutenant Duley introduced himself, returning the salute with a relaxed precision that spoke of experience.

"I suspect this is your first time in the F-4, so let me tell you a little about it." His tone was matter-of-fact but not condescending.

Duley led Phillip out to the jet, the heat from the tarmac rising in visible waves around them. The Phantom loomed before them—fifty-eight feet of lethal aeronautical engineering.

"She's not pretty like those Air Force toys, but she'll get us home," Duley said with evident pride, patting the fuselage.

As they circled the aircraft, Duley methodically explained the features of the rear cockpit where Phillip would be sitting—the rudimentary flight controls, which he was not to touch, the various gauges, and the communication systems. He emphasized the safety items with particular care: the emergency oxygen supply, the survival kit stowed beneath the seat, and seat ejection control.

"Two things you absolutely need to remember," Duley said, holding up two fingers for emphasis. "First, this is the ejection handle." He pointed to a yellow and black striped loop between Phillip's legs. "Pull it only if you see me eject first or if I give the order.

"Second," he continued, his expression lightening slightly. "Don't puke in my back seat. If you feel it coming, there's a bag in the left pocket by your knee. Use it. We're flying a multi-million-dollar war machine, not a flying head."

With the briefing complete, a ground crew member helped Phillip climb up the ladder and lower himself into the rear cockpit. The seat was surprisingly comfortable, but constraining. The crew chief efficiently secured Phillip's harness, cinching the straps until they bit into his shoulders—uncomfortable but reassuring. The helmet and oxygen mask felt alien and claustrophobic as the canopy settled over his head.

Lieutenant Duley climbed into the front seat with practiced ease, his movements economical and confident. After a brief communication with the tower, he began taxiing toward the runway. Phillip watched as the world outside became a blur of colors and shapes.

"Tower has cleared us for immediate takeoff," Duley's voice came through the headset, surprisingly clear despite the ambient noise. "We'll be doing a combat departure—

standard procedure in a hot zone like this. That means we go vertical as soon as we're wheels up to avoid any surface-to-air threats and reach cruising altitude quickly. You ready for this, sailor?"

Before Phillip could fully process what 'combat departure' meant, the Lieutenant pushed the throttles forward. The engines roared with unleashed power, and the Phantom surged down the runway, pressing Phillip back into his seat with unexpected force.

"Holy shit!" came out of Phillip's mouth as he was pushed back in his seat like someone was sitting on his chest. His eyes were watering, and the skin on his face was pulled back as they climbed. He could see nothing but blue sky until they leveled off at 20,000 feet.

Once leveled off, the pilot said, "You good?" to which Phillip gave the thumbs up, still trying to catch his breath.

"Okay, we are going to be cruising at 517 knots (595 mph), so we should catch up with the ship in a couple of hours."

Phillip looked out of the cockpit at the blue water below as he and Lieutenant Duley had a brief conversation about nothing in particular, just to break the boredom of a long flight.

Time passed as Phillip gazed out the window. Finally, the pilot said, "The nest is on your starboard side."

Phillip looked to the horizon, seeing the carrier below. "Damn, it doesn't look so big from up here."

The lieutenant laughed and said, "Wait until you see her on approach."

As he made a roll, coming out of the marshal stack, Phillip wanted to reach for something to hold, but knew better. The pilot was quickly getting the rhythm of the ship as he listened to the LSO.

"Quarter mile, call the ball."

"Ball," the pilot responded as he gained speed to come aboard. The pilot touched down on the deck, and the tail hook engaged a wire, causing a sudden deceleration that felt like hitting a wall. The plane was quickly brought to a stop, with both of them feeling a strong forward impact as the arresting gear absorbed the energy.

The cable was disconnected as the pilot raised his wings and came to a stop. Chocks were placed under the wheels as the cockpit opened.

"Your home," the lieutenant said.

Phillip released the restraints that had held him in place, removed his helmet, and climbed down to the deck. Phillip thanked him for the ride, but in his mind, he was thinking, "Home? Not yet."

Phillip went to his birthing area to get out of his flight suit and change into his dungarees. Carlos, who was lying on his rack, sat up. "You're back?"

Phillip made eye contact and said, "The next time I volunteer please slap the shit out of me."

Carlos laughed, saying, "It was that bad? Tell me all about it."

As Phillip put on his shirt, he said, "Later, but now I need to check in with the Chief and get some coffee. You want to come?"

Carlos jumped down, saying, "Sure, I can buy, and you can tell me all about your time in Da Nang."

Phillip said it sounded good, but he needed to stop at the ship's store to get a carton of Marlboros.

"Did you know they raised the price?" Phillip asked.

"How much are they now? "They're now $1.20 a carton."

Phillip laughed, saying, "If they keep raising their prices, I think I'll need to switch to a pipe."

The sick bay was empty, so everyone on duty was just sitting around playing cards, drinking coffee, or writing letters. Phillip told everyone about his month in Da Nang, the big-ass Gunnery Sergeant, and their patrols.

They all grew quiet when Phillip mentioned the young Marine he lost. The room fell silent except for the distant hum of the ship's engines. The Chief, a man with eyes that had seen too much, saw the question in Phillip's eyes, saying, "That's tough, but I'm sure you did everything you could. Sometimes the best medicine in the world can't save them."

Phillip thought, 'Rule number 2.'

The conversation switched to Japan and the scuttlebutt going around about Admiral Elmo R. "Bud" Zumwalt, Jr., who had assumed command of the 7th Fleet on July 7, 1970, coming aboard.

"That makes sense," Johansen said as he finished his coffee, "Why else are we spit-shining this damn boat again?"

The Chief smiled and replied, "Maybe to keep you from getting bored."

The USS Midway pulled into Yokosuka Naval Base as the late afternoon sun glinted off the water. Most of the sailors were given 72-hour liberty passes. Phillip, Wilson, Martinez, and Johansen grabbed their overnight bags and headed down the gangway.

The four friends caught the express train into Tokyo, watching the landscape transform from industrial port to dense urban sprawl. Martinez pressed his face against the window as Tokyo Tower came into view, its orange and white spire piercing the sky.

"There it is," Wilson said, pointing. "The same tower where Tokyo Rose broadcast her propaganda to American troops during World War II."

They checked into a hotel near the tower, two sailors to a room. After freshening up, they decided to keep their dress whites on because they hadn't bothered to pack much civilian clothing.

"Let's hit the Ginza," Phillip suggested. "Supposed to be the Times Square of Tokyo."

The Ginza district bustled with more people than any of them had ever seen in one place. The streets were so packed that vehicles were prohibited. Neon signs in

Japanese characters illuminated buildings that seemed to stretch endlessly upward.

As they turned a corner, Martinez suddenly stopped and grinned. "You've got to be kidding me."

There, amidst the foreign landscape of Tokyo, stood the familiar golden arches of McDonald's. They looked at each other and laughed before heading inside without discussion. The restaurant was packed with locals, and the four Americans ordered the closest thing to home they could find—Big Mac meals with large Cokes.

With no tables available, they took their food outside and sat on the curb. Phillip savored a fry, closing his eyes. "Man, I never thought McDonald's would taste this good."

As they ate, they gradually became aware of curious stares. A large crowd of Japanese citizens had gathered nearby, several taking pictures with cameras that hung around their necks.

"Did we become famous?" Carlos asked mid-bite.

Phillip didn't even look up from his fries. "Nah, but we'll probably end up on someone's coffee table soon.

Johansen waved at a young Japanese couple who

bowed slightly in return. They wandered through the district, marveling at the chaos of lights, sounds, and the organized bustle of thousands of people moving with purpose.

"This is wild," Johansen said, looking up at a massive video screen displaying a Japanese commercial featuring what appeared to be a singing cat.

It was getting late, and fatigue began to set in. They headed back to their hotel, the Tokyo Tower now illuminated in brilliant light against the night sky.

"Mount Fuji tomorrow, they say we need to get an early start," Phillip said as they entered the hotel lobby.

Martinez yawned in agreement. "Never thought I'd climb a volcano in Japan."

"Technically, it's a dormant stratovolcano," Wilson corrected, earning him a punch in the arm.

The next day, they got up early and had a traditional Japanese breakfast of steamed rice, miso soup, pickled vegetables (tsukemono), and green tea. After breakfast, they took a train to Mount Fuji, riding alongside locals heading to work and schoolchildren in their blue uniforms and backpacks. They transferred to a local bus for the final leg of the journey.

Taking 2½ hours to reach the mountain base, they realized they wouldn't have time to climb to the top. The Yoshida Trail would take a little longer than 5 hours to ascend, so instead, they took pictures, mingled with the Japanese and visitors who had come to make the climb, and simply enjoyed their day admiring Japan's most iconic natural landmark.

Wilson observed, "They sure bow a lot," not yet understanding that bowing is a fundamental greeting and expression of respect in Japanese culture, often accompanied by saying "konnichiwa" (hello/good afternoon), or other appropriate greetings such as "hi." One older gentleman, appreciating their respectful attitude toward the sacred mountain, gifted them walking sticks, called "kongō-zue," traditionally stamped at stations along the climbing route. He bowed, saying, *"Anata no sonkei ni kansha shimasu. Watashi mo anata ni keii o arawashimasu."* Translation: 'Thank you for your respect. I give mine to you.' They accepted the gift and bowed back, showing their gratitude.

As they gazed up at the perfect cone of the mountain, they learned that Mount Fuji, or "Fuji-San" as the Japanese call it, is not just a natural wonder but a spiritual symbol deeply embedded in Japanese culture and art for centuries.

After making it back to Tokyo, they spent one more evening walking around, taking in the sights and observing the people as they went about their way. The energy of the city at dusk was mesmerizing—businessmen loosening their ties as they headed to after-work gatherings, young couples strolling hand in hand.

Later, they wandered through Ginza, watching street performers. They stopped to watch a woman in a traditional kimono carefully navigate the modern streets. Her presence was a living embodiment of Japan's beautiful contradiction of honoring tradition and embracing modernity.

Their final nightcap came at a hidden bar. They slowly sipped their drinks while looking out the windows, which offered a breathtaking panorama of Tokyo's endless sea of lights.

In the morning, they checked out of the hotel and caught the train back to the port where their ship awaited them. The staff at the hotel bowed deeply as they departed, a gesture they now understood represented courtesy and sincere appreciation for their visit.

As they made the final steps toward the ship, Phillip

said, "Next time I want to come during cherry blossom season and stay long enough to make that climb."

Wilson agreed. He also wanted to come back. Boarding the ship may have marked the end of their journey, but the memories would remain with them for a lifetime.

Chapter 24: Crossroads at Sea

As the ship cut through the waters of the Pacific, Phillip retreated to his bunk and read through the letters awaiting his arrival back on board—something to focus on besides the constant hum of engines and the stale air.

Charlie had written that her grandmother was ill. She was considering leaving the University of San Francisco to transfer to the University of Hawaii and complete her Bachelor's degree in nursing. She wanted to be close to her grandmother, who was born in Kyoto before the war and had been her rock and confidante.

Charlie didn't want to waste a minute being so far away, especially now that the doctors were using words like "progressive" and "uncertain."

"Besides, I will get to see you sooner when you stop here and introduce you to her. She's always asking about 'that nice Navy boy.' Says she can tell from your photo that you have a good heart."

Phillip ran his thumb over the edge of the photograph Charlie had included—a photo of the ship passing under the

Golden Gate Bridge with Phillip standing on the flight deck, waving as they passed under it on their way to sea.

He wrote back late into the night, telling her all about Japan and the impression it had on him, the respectful bow of the people, the photo event on the Ginza, and the beauty of Mount Fuji. He described the ancient temples and gardens they passed on their way to Mount Fuji, as well as the kindness of the people they met.

He knew he could not divulge the ship's movements—security protocols were strict—but wasn't sure they would make a stop in Hawaii. Their departure was several months out, and things could change. And he didn't want to think about saying goodbye in a letter. Some goodbyes needed to be conveyed through more than just ink on paper.

He discovered that his parents knew he had left the ship and was in Da Nang. He figured his writings must have given it away, or perhaps it was simply a mother's intuition. Now, he could finally write to them, explaining that he was safely back on the ship. In his letter, he made sure to apologize for not being upfront with her earlier—he had only wanted to spare her from the additional worry he knew she would feel.

The Midway steamed towards Yankee Station, where the USS Ranger was waiting for her arrival and heading back to the States. The scuttlebutt about the Admiral coming aboard was no longer rumor but fact, as the sailors on the ship were preparing for his arrival. Floors looked like glass; the brass was polished so well that you could use it to shave. All ropes were replaced, and the decks, quarters, and mess area were ready.

Phillip watched from his station as the Admiral came aboard with little fanfare. As he stepped from the helicopter, he was greeted by the captain and several senior officers. After exchanging salutes, he was whisked away to the island where he would be shown the admiral's quarters. The boatswain's mate announced his arrival, along with a signal that a man was aloft changing out the signal flags, indicating that, for now, Midway was the flagship.

The various flags flying on the mast are known as Signal Flags. They represent letters, numbers, and a few other things. They are used to send messages, and each flag or set of flags has its own meaning.

The ship went about its day, preparing to enter the Tonkin Gulf and return to the reason it was there. Except for an occasional announcement that the Admiral was on the bridge, they didn't even know he was there.

It was past midnight as Phillip started his day, crossing

the flight deck and heading up to Air Operations to obtain that day's flight plan. The deck vibrated beneath his feet, a reminder of the ship's living, breathing nature—even in the deepest hours of the night.

As he climbed the stairs going up to the bridge, he noticed that both the Captain and Rear Admiral Elmo Zumwalt Jr., the 19th and youngest Chief of Naval Operations and a highly decorated veteran of World War II, were awake and engaged in an intense but pleasant conversation as they studied navigation screens and the soft glow of maritime instruments.

He slipped into Air Operations, retrieved the flight plans, and as he walked out, he had to give way, pressing himself against the bulkhead to allow the senior officers to pass. He stood at attention while they moved, not rendering a salute because they were at sea and not wearing covers. This subtle but important maritime protocol spoke to the unique world of naval service.

The Admiral's eyes met Phillip's for a brief moment. "Good morning, Corpsman," Zumwalt said, his voice carrying the quiet authority of a man who had seen it all and was reshaping the Navy.

"Good morning, Admiral," Phillip responded, his voice

crisp and respectful.

Zumwalt was more than just another senior officer. He was a legend in the making—a commander who was fundamentally changing the face of the United States Navy. His recent Z-grams had been revolutionary, challenging centuries of racial segregation and discrimination within the military ranks. Phillip had heard whispers of these changes, of how Zumwalt was fighting battles both on and off the ship.

As the Admiral and Captain continued down the corridor, Phillip's mind raced. This was the 7th Fleet Commander—a man who had earned a Bronze Star and a Silver Star in World War II, who was now steering the Navy through the complex waters of the Vietnam War and social change.

As he descended to the hangar deck, passing by aircraft that were secured, looking like sleeping giants waiting for dawn's first light, he walked into the galley. Phillip grabbed a tray of strong coffee, powdered eggs, fried potatoes, bacon that was almost done, and toast that had apparently spent too much time in the toaster.

As he sat down, keeping his arms on both sides of the tray to prevent it from sliding down the table, he smiled to himself. One day, he would tell his grandchildren about this night.

Around 0200, a call came in from the destroyer assigned to their task force over the ship-to-ship radio. The voice cut through the quiet of an early morning routine. The destroyer's mission was primarily focused on anti-submarine warfare, anti-surface warfare, and anti-air warfare. It served as the carrier's defensive bubble, protecting it from surface and air threats, potentially even engaging enemy ships or aircraft. Everyone in sick bay listened carefully as they tried to wake up and prepare for the day.

"School boy, school boy," the ship's handle echoed through their room like a ghost calling out from deep in the ocean. The radio operator's voice was tense, professional, but with an undercurrent of urgency that every seasoned sailor recognized. "We have an injured seaman who needs to be transferred to your ship for medical treatment. He's stabilized but needs surgical intervention."

Chief Mitchell began barking orders, transforming the sleepy sick bay into a hive of purposeful activity. "Martinez, get the blood bank ready—we might need it. Johansen, prepare the OR."

Phillip would be on the flight deck observing the morning flight operations and keeping a watchful eye out for any medical problems.

At dawn, the destroyer pulled alongside the carrier as it was tossing around like a toy in a bathtub. The sea had grown restless overnight, heavy swells lifting and dropping both massive warships in an unnerving dance. The morning sky was clear, but it offered no comfort to the men preparing for the dangerous transfer.

The boatswain's mate fired a line across the bow with the precision of an archer, the thin rope arcing through the misty air before landing perfectly on the destroyer's deck. Sailors on both vessels moved with precision—this was a dangerous maneuver in calm seas, and today the ocean was anything but calm.

The line was secured, and the sailor, strapped to a gurney, was carefully pulled from one ship to the other, suspended momentarily above the churning gap between vessels—thirty feet of sea that could claim a life in seconds if anything went wrong. Phillip watched from the sickbay station on the ship's TV.

Once on board, he was rushed to sick bay and the awaiting doctors. Phillip caught a glimpse of the injured sailor, young, maybe nineteen, face pale and drawn with pain despite the morphine. Another kid, not much different from himself, who had a compound fracture to his tibia that was going to need surgery. Phillip knew he wouldn't be scrubbing in for this one, as air operations would commence as soon as the destroyer was back in place.

The destroyer fell back into position behind the carrier, readying itself for air operations to begin. From the flight deck, Phillip could see it taking its place, following the carrier's wake.

Almadova looked at Phillip and said, "This is going to be a long day. With this delay, we'll be catching birds after sunset."

There was a hint of excitement in his voice that Phillip recognized immediately—flight operations were a dangerous mission during daylight hours, but now it would take everyone's focus to be performed in the dark.

Phillip knew he would be off duty at noon, but he was hoping to get a closer look at night operations. The Air Boss's vantage point would be out of the question because the Admiral would be watching from there, but perhaps he could find a spot on the island structure with a good view of the flight deck.

The ship turned into the wind, preparing for the day's first launch. Pilots checked their planes as ordnance handlers attached weapons they would need for today's mission under their wings.

Phillip watched, thinking, 'Just another day in the United States Navy,' as he placed his headset over his ears.

The time had come for the Admiral to leave the ship and head back to Dixie Station. The ship's intercom crackled to life.

"This is the Admiral speaking. As I prepare to depart, I want to express my deepest gratitude for your service and the professional manner in which you've conducted Navy business."

Every sailor's attention was turned to the voice coming into their living and work stations. Nothing or no one moved as they listened to the voice of their fleet commander.

"Remember this," the Admiral continued, his voice carrying the weight of experience. "The best warships in the world are of no avail without the crews, like the one I see here today, to sail and fight on them." He paused briefly, then concluded with the traditional naval sign-off: "That is all."

On the flight deck, the helicopter sat awaiting the Admiral's arrival. The boatswain's pipe sounded—the high, warbling tone that had signaled naval ceremony for centuries—as the Admiral emerged onto the deck. He exchanged final salutes with the ship's captain and senior officers before boarding the helicopter.

As the aircraft lifted from the deck, the ship's speakers came alive once more: "Man aloft! Do not rotate or radiate! Man aloft!" The warning echoed across the decks, ensuring all radar and communication equipment remained dormant as a signalman high on the ship's mast began changing the seven-starred pennant of the 7th Fleet Commander departing. The new flags snapped in the sea breeze, a visible announcement to all vessels in the area that the ship no longer carried the Fleet Commander.

As they got closer to the end of the ship's tour, Phillip was also getting close to the end of his active duty commitment. The realization brought mixed emotions—relief mingled with uncertainty about what civilian life would hold after two years at sea. The USS Midway had become home, its routines and rhythms as familiar to him as breathing. Chief Mitchell, noticing Phillip's distracted gaze across the endless Pacific, told him he needed to go down to see Processing, who would explain his options.

Phillip descended three ladder wells to the administrative

deck, the temperature rising with each level. He paused briefly outside the processing office, taking a deep breath of recycled ship air tinged with the faint smell of cigarettes and coffee. Phillip entered the small, cramped processing room, where a 2nd class petty officer was banging away on a typewriter, the clacking keys echoing off the metal bulkheads. The young Petty Officer turned and asked if he could help. Phillip wiped the sweat from his brow, told the petty officer why he was there, and was directed to take a seat on a hard folding chair that had probably been in service longer than he'd been alive.

"Name and service number?" the petty officer asked without looking up, fingers poised over the typewriter keys.

"McManus, B863071," Phillip answered.

After shuffling through some paperwork, finding his folder that contained the sum total of Phillip's naval career, the petty officer turned to Phillip and said, "Okay, you are scheduled to be separated on November 30. Here are your options." He spoke with the efficiency of someone who'd delivered this speech dozens of times before.

Phillip leaned forward. Options? The word sparked a glimmer of hope he hadn't expected to feel.

Petty Officer Ness, his nameplate catching the light as he shifted in his chair, said, "Upon arrival back to Alameda, you can be discharged with no commitment to any additional reserve training, or you can ship over for another 6 years and start a career in the Navy." He paused, watching Phillip's reaction before continuing, "If you do reenlist while in this combat zone, you will receive a $10,000 bonus, paid in equal amounts each year over the length of your new enlistment. That amount will be tax-free if you can give me your answer before we leave Yankee Station."

The sum hung in the air between them. Ten thousand dollars was no small amount. Phillip's mind raced, calculating possibilities he hadn't considered before walking into this room.

"Can I stay on sea duty?" Phillip asked, surprising himself with the question. The thought of leaving the ocean, of no longer falling asleep to the gentle rocking of the ship, suddenly seemed more daunting than he'd anticipated.

Ness looked at him, his expression suggesting he'd heard this request before. "No, you have spent all your two years on sea duty, so you will need to go to shore duty, a station of your choosing."

Phillip tried to barter for an assignment to the USS

Kennedy and a tour of the Mediterranean, painting a picture of himself sailing into exotic ports he'd only seen in magazines. Ness listened politely but shook his head at that suggestion, his expression making it clear that regulations weren't open to negotiation.

"I guess I need to think about it," Phillip finally said, deflating slightly as the reality of his limited choices sank in. The weight of the decision pressed on him—six more years committed to the Navy versus stepping into the uncertain civilian world.

"Your choice," Ness said with a shrug that suggested he'd seen sailors struggle with this decision countless times before. "But I need an answer in a couple of weeks for the bonus, or at least by the 10th of November." He slid a form across the desk. "Take this, read it over. Talk to some of the career men if you're on the fence."

Phillip thanked Petty Officer Ness as he headed back to sick bay, clutching the paperwork that represented his future. The form felt heavier than its single sheet suggested. As he made his way through the narrow passageways back to sick bay, he looked past familiar faces he'd served alongside.

When he walked in, Chief Mitchell looked up from his coffee cup. "Well? Are you staying in the Navy or going back to being a civilian?" The question hung in the air, weighted with all the implications of choosing one life over another.

Phillip slumped into the chair across from the Chief's desk, removing his ball cap as he explained the options he was given. "I don't get it. Why can't I take some poor, married sailors' sea duty so they can stay with their family?" His voice showed his frustration.

The chief set his coffee cup down and said, "Trying to apply logic to Navy regulations would only give you a headache. Hell, I have been in twenty-three years, and I still don't understand half the decisions that come down from above."

Phillip, looking nowhere in particular, said, "I love the Navy and being at sea, but I'm not sure my enthusiasm would be the same if I were landlocked for two years. I guess I've got something to sleep on."

Chief Mitchell leaned back in his chair. His eyes had seen generations of sailors come and go. "You're a good corpsman, McManus. You'd be an asset to any command you would be assigned to. But I've seen enough men reenlist for the wrong reasons. You have to decide if the Navy is the right fit for you."

Chief took another sip of his coffee, then added, "And let's be honest, with your skills, you could probably walk into any hospital back home and make twice what Uncle Sam pays you."

Phillip nodded, absorbing the Chief's words. He had two weeks to decide what he wanted his future to look like.

Chapter 25: The Long Way Back Home

As the last plane landed aboard, you could almost hear the ship give a sigh of relief. It was over—mission complete, time to go home.

Phillip removed his headset and looked around, taking in the moment. Across the flight deck, sailors exchanged handshakes and pats on the back as they finished their tasks and disappeared into the depths of the carrier. The massive ship beneath them had carried them through months of combat operations, and now it would carry them home.

"Mission complete," Phillip whispered to himself, the words barely audible above the dying whine of aircraft engines.

They had flown over 228 sorties, dropping 750,000 pounds of ordnance over North Vietnam, Laos, and Cambodia. Almost every aircraft had returned safely, all but two. On October 19th, they'd lost an E-2B Hawkeye when it collided with an A-7 on final approach. The A-7 had crossed the landing pattern and struck the Hawkeye's wing, causing a catastrophic loss of hydraulic pressure and control. All five crew members aboard the E-2B were lost to the depths. The A-7 pilot had ejected and was recovered by the rescue helicopter, but the Hawkeye crew now rested eternally in Davy Jones' locker, joining countless brothers-in-arms who had gone before them.

There had been other close calls—aircraft damaged from small arms fire, hung ordnance, accidents to crew—but this one lingered on Phillip's mind. They were so close to getting to go home. And there was nothing to send home to those who were waiting for them. Little did they know that when they said goodbye in San Diego, it would be the last time they would see, hold, or hear their voices again. Rule number one also applied at sea.

As the flight deck cleared and the ship turned toward home waters, Phillip couldn't help but think of those five men. Their absence was a reminder of the cost that always came with duty. Yet the mission was complete, and for most aboard, tomorrow would bring another sunrise, another day closer to home.

The carrier pushed forward through the deep blue

waters, its massive wake stretching back toward the war they were leaving behind.

That evening, down on the hangar deck, they were going to show the movie "MASH." Phillip, Johansen, Martinez, Manu, and Wilson found a spot and took a seat. As the movie ran, the boys laughed out loud; being Corpsmen, they saw the humor in the film that others might miss.

Phillip looked at Wilson and said, "That's you running the martini parties."

Johansen nudged Phillip with his elbow. "And you would be doing the practical joker."

Manu shook his head, grinning. "I'd be Radar, always knowing what the Commander wants before he even asks."

"Who would I be?" Carlos asked.

"You're definitely Trapper," Phillip said. "Always trying to charm the girls when we're in port."

The movie continued, and their laughter occasionally drew looks from the sailors seated nearby. Most of the crew enjoyed the film, but the medical team caught on to the inside jokes and gallows humor unique to their profession.

The four friends enjoyed the rest of the movie,

occasionally whispering comparisons between their real-life experiences and the fictionalized ones on screen.

As they walked back to their quarters, the four continued their banter, their friendship forged through shared experiences both mundane and extraordinary. The movie had been entertaining, but the real story was the bond between them—navy corpsmen carrying on a proud tradition of service, sacrifice, and the occasional well-executed pranks.

The next stop was Hong Kong, a place for a little R&R, but mostly to start the transition from a combat role back to peacetime life as a sailor. The city was a modern-day complex seamlessly mixed with ancient structures from the past, a dazzling display of the collision of eras.

Standing amid the bustling streets, Phillip and Carlos marveled at the "Monster Building" in Quarry Bay, a complex of five densely packed, interconnected towers that resembled a concrete beehive. These structures were renowned for their unique architectural style. And rumor had it that this one particular tower marked one floor for each of the owner's wives—a tale that sailors repeated, whether true or not.

From the harbor, they watched sampans navigating

around massive freighters that were unloading their merchandise to the duty-free port. The small wooden boats darted between ships, their operators skillfully steering with single oars, having mastered this dance through generations. Floating restaurants, adorned with red lanterns and gold dragons, bobbed gently on the water, offering an authentic taste of Cantonese cuisine as the charm of old Hong Kong mingled with its modern counterpart.

Taking advantage of the favorable exchange rate between the US dollar and the Hong Kong dollar, Phillip bought his first Seiko watch, some Noritake China, and a reel-to-reel tape deck—luxuries that seemed almost impossible to get were quite affordable here. He also picked up a jewelry box for Anna, featuring a rickshaw runner, which played a delicate tune when the lid was opened. For Jim, he found a handmade pipe cut from monkey pod, its grain polished to a rich, honey-colored finish.

"These people probably think we're rich the way we're spending our money," Carlos observed, watching shopkeepers eagerly recommend additional items.

"Yeah, if they only knew how long we've had to save our pay, they might understand," Phillip replied. "But we've probably spent more than most locals would make in a year."

They spent a couple of nights enjoying traditional meals served in restaurants that normally didn't see sailors—establishments tucked away in side streets where the food was authentic and the atmosphere more traditional. They tried to pick items from menus based on pictures since they obviously couldn't read Chinese, leading to some surprising but mostly delicious discoveries. They traveled around the city in rickshaws, the drivers weaving expertly through narrow streets while pointing out landmarks in broken English, and drank what the locals called beer, lighter than what they were used to, but refreshing anyway.

Their time in port came to an end too quickly. On their final day, they took the dinghy back to their ship with their treasured purchases carefully wrapped and stored away until they got home. As the shoreline of Hong Kong receded behind them, the towering skyline etched itself into their memories—another port, another story to tell.

Lieutenant Hayes, in the weather room, squinted at the radar screen, his weathered face tightening with concern. They were about 100 nautical miles out from the Philippines.

He contacted the bridge, telling the captain that the storm system had intensified to typhoon status. "We can't outrun it now, and we can't go back."

The skipper acknowledged the report as he reached for the intercom. His voice echoed throughout the massive aircraft carrier: "All hands, turn to. Secure all planes and equipment. Button down the hatches and make preparations for a typhoon that is rapidly approaching that we cannot steer clear of."

The 5,000-strong crew sprang into action. Petty Officer Rodriguez, who'd been through two typhoons before, felt the familiar knot in his stomach as he directed his aviation team in securing the aircraft with additional chains. "Double-check everything!" he shouted over the increasing wind. "This isn't going to be a gentle ride!"

Aircraft carriers are designed to withstand harsh weather, but this typhoon would pose significant challenges to their operation and structural integrity. The potential for flight deck damage, aircraft damage, and even capsizing was uncertain. It would test the skills and durability of this ship, which was now adrift amongst the hollows of a storm that meteorologists had named "Rose."

The first massive wave hit shortly after 1600 hrs. A thunderous crash followed the roar of water cascading across the decks. High waves crashed over the ship, soaking the hangar deck and spilling down the hatches to lower decks.

Waves so big they came over the bow, striking the windows of the bridge with enough force to make even the seasoned helmsman flinch.

"Hold her steady!" the captain commanded, gripping the console as the ship listed fifteen degrees to port.

Below decks, unsecured items were tossed around like clothes in a dryer. The sickening smell of vomit mingled with the damp odor of seawater in compartments that were supposed to stay dry. Every man not needed was securely in their racks, being held in place by their seatbelts, many murmuring prayers.

For six grueling hours, the ship fought its way through the storm, the winds reaching 100 miles per hour. The ship growled as it took punches and rolls of 24 degrees. For a brief period, there was an eerie calm as they passed through the eye, then the storm came rushing back with more force and determination to take this ship out. But it fought back, coming out of it and into calmer seas. The crash of waves and the howling wind gradually subsided until a strange quiet settled over the carrier.

When the all-clear finally sounded, the crew, those who

were not seasick, emerged to inspect the ship. Each surveyed the damage as the ship settled back into a gentler rocking motion, one they were accustomed to through dissipating clouds. They discovered minimal structural damage. Everyone was fine, with some sailors who were needed on duty receiving bruises and minor cuts as they tried to stay on their feet and carry out their mission throughout the ordeal.

"The ship held together," the skipper nodded, pride evident in his voice. "She's a tough old bird."

The Philippines didn't fare as well. Typhoon Rose caused extensive damage across the central islands, destroying thousands of homes and killing over 130 people. Within hours of clearing the storm,

Phillip and Manu, after cleaning up the sick bay, putting medical supplies back in the cabinets that had flown open, and clearing up any mess the storm had left behind, made their way up to the catwalk. It was after midnight; their shift was over. As they gazed out to see the sky filling with stars and a moon hiding behind a cloud, Phillip looked to the heavens and said, "Anything else I need to see before I make my decision?"

"Still glad you joined the Navy?" Petty Officer Manu

asked.

Without looking, Phillip said, "Yes, but after today, I am not sure I want to go back to sea. I thought we were goners." He went on to ask Manu, "How do you do it, how do you get this close to people, then in two years they expect you to just start over?"

Manu paused and said, "It just is a part of Navy life."

The next point that would signal how much further they had to go was the International Date Line. As they crossed over it, Tuesday magically transformed back into Monday.

Wilson's eyes lit up with mischief. "I guess we won't have to clean the ship today," he declared triumphantly, "we already did it yesterday... which is technically today... which is now yesterday again!"

Just as the last word left his mouth, the boatswain's whistle shrieked through the air: "Sweepers, sweepers, man your brooms and clean the ship fore and aft!"

The Chief erupted in laughter at Wilson's facial expression. "There's your answer, sailor. The Navy, where you can time travel and still not escape chores."

He gave Wilson a consoling pat on the shoulder. "But I

hear we're having steak tonight... for the second time this Monday."

Charlie had transferred schools, and the ship would not be stopping in Hawaii, sticking to its original plan. The Navy wanted to get the crew home for Thanksgiving. Philip approached the Chief, concerned about protocol. "Would I be breaking any rules if I mentioned our itinerary in a letter?"

The Chief nodded thoughtfully. "It's okay to mention we're skipping Hawaii, but keep our Alameda arrival date to yourself."

Philip wrote the letter, knowing she probably wouldn't receive it until after they'd already returned to port. He only had her dorm room phone number, and with his decision to accept discharge, this was essentially goodbye.

As he wrote, he thought about her with gratitude. She had given him something normal to hold onto during an abnormal time in his life. She had spoken of her dreams to live in the islands, while he longed to return to the familiar comfort of Iowa. Their paths were clearly diverging. She had wished him well, promising to treasure their shared moments in San Francisco. Phillip got the life lesson that you don't always get to say goodbye.

On Phillip's last night aboard the ship, he was unable to sleep. The gentle rocking that had once lulled him to rest now kept him wide awake. His mind was too full of memories. He wandered down to sick bay, a place that had consumed so much of his time.

As he sat there in the dim light, he looked around, reliving the past year and all the people who had come into his life—people he had since said goodbye to. The echoes of their laughter seemed to bounce off the steel walls, ghostly reminders of moments now passed.

People who were strangers a year ago had become family. People who knew more about him than most of his own relatives. They had shared meals in the mess hall, stood shoulder to shoulder during storms, exchanged stories during long nights, and supported each other in the chaos on the flight deck. They had seen it all: his happiness, his sadness, his best moments, and the times when he was broken. They had picked him up when he faltered and celebrated his triumphs.

They all had dispersed, each returning to separate lives and distant homes. These were people he would never see again, but could never forget—they were now woven permanently into the fabric of who he had become.

The day finally came. Countless crew members stood shoulder to shoulder on the flight deck, straining their eyes toward the horizon until they spotted it—the Golden Gate Bridge gleaming in the California sunshine, a brilliant announcement that they were home. Phillip thought about how his father had described seeing the Statue of Liberty when returning from his own deployment. In that moment, he understood the profound relief his dad must have felt, that universal homecoming emotion that transcends generations of servicemen.

As tugboats nudged their massive vessel toward the pier, a Navy band played triumphantly, announcing their return. Once the ship docked and gangways locked into place, men practically flew off the deck and into the waiting arms of families—wives clutching children, parents with tear-streaked faces, all those connections that were severed ten months ago now joyfully restored.

Phillip watched the reunions from the flight deck, a bittersweet observer. His own welcome would have to wait—five more days of processing and duties before he could finally set foot in Iowa. But even at a distance, witnessing these moments of pure joy made the anticipation of his own homecoming all the sweeter.

As Phillip walked down the gangway for the last time, seabag slung over his shoulder, the sound of metal beneath his feet was like a farewell whisper from the ship that had been his home. The weight of the canvas against his back was familiar—comforting even—but lighter somehow than when he'd first boarded months ago. What he carried now wasn't measured in pounds of clothing and necessities, but in memories that had no physical form yet felt heavier than any anchor.

His thoughts turned to the adventure from which he was returning, not as a coherent narrative but as fragments of sensation that defied chronology—the taste of salt that never quite left his lips, the way his body had learned to sway with the rhythm of waves until stillness felt foreign.

Pausing at the bottom of the gangway, he looked back at the weathered hull rising above him.

How does one explain the voyage and the tranquil peace that washes over you while lying in a hammock, gazing into a night sky so vast and distant that not even God could have found you?

What he felt and what he saw existed beyond the realm of words. Language was a net with holes too wide to catch the fish of his experience. The moonless night, dolphins that were so close he could hear them whistle while swimming alongside. The storm that had humbled them all, and how afterwards, the world seemed reborn, cleansed.

But the emotions would remain with him, dormant perhaps, but never truly forgotten, resurfacing every time he gazed out across the endless blue of the ocean.

He took his first steps onto solid ground, and the earth felt like a stranger. His sea legs still compensated for a roll that was no longer there, making him sway slightly, like a man caught between worlds. Behind him lay the ship, before him the rest of his life. Phillip adjusted his seabag, squared his shoulders against the weight of return, and set his course toward home, carrying within him an ocean he could never fully share but would never willingly surrender.

Phillip turned 21 on their way home, so he decided to go down to the wine cellar he and Charlie had visited before leaving the city. He ordered some wine and let the soft music wash over him, thoughts drifting to the city by the bay. San Francisco had become a part of him now. One last bowl of steaming clam chowder in a sourdough bread bowl, one more cable car ride, then off to the airport to go home.

At the airport, there were protesters. They weren't just protesting the war but were screaming obscenities at those who had participated in it.

"Baby killer!" someone shouted, though Phillip had never fired a shot in anger. He kept his head down and walked at a quicker pace. Now he understood why it was suggested to put on civilian clothes before arriving. But Phillip was proud of his service and wasn't going to let someone who knew nothing about him change that. His fingers instinctively touched the dog tags hidden beneath his shirt—a reminder of who he really was.

His flight arrived in Des Moines around 7 PM. Anna and Jim came rushing up to him, giving him hugs, handshakes, and pats on the back. It was his time to be welcomed home, and it was perfect.

Anna, tears streaming unchecked down her weathered cheeks, cupped Phillip's face between her soft hands. Her voice broke as she searched his gaze.

"Son," she whispered. "Your eyes no longer shine because they can't hide what you've seen, and others can only see they've changed. I saw it in Jim when he came home, and now it's a part of who you are." Her thumb gently wiped away a tear he hadn't realized he'd shed. "You won't need to explain, but you will need to make peace with it."

Once they got into Ottumwa, Phillip asked if the canteen was still open. Jim checked his watch, confirming they were.

"Can we stop?" Phillip asked.

"I don't see any reason we can't, now that we have no place to go but home," Jim replied.

As they parked the car and walked toward the canteen, Anna lingered a step behind her son. Her throat tightened, not with fear as it had for so many endless months, but with a gratitude so intense it was almost painful. The war continued for others, but for Anna, the unbearable vigil had finally come to an end. God had returned all her boys to her. She finally felt a mother's peace, no more countless sleepless nights and silent tears, recognizable only to those who had lived with the constant fear that their children might never come home; some didn't. Her boys came home. Hopefully, to less turbulent times than they had shared growing up in the 60s.

Afterword

A Sailor's Journey Home

As I sit here in the twilight of my years, watching the sunset paint the Arizona sky from my patio, my mind often wanders back through our family's journey. It's been a long voyage from those days aboard the aircraft carrier to these peaceful days of retirement.

My journey since walking off the Midway took more turns than I could have imagined as a young sailor. After the Navy, I found work at Saint Joseph Hospital, where I moved between the ER, ICU, and surgical suite, always drawn to helping others in their moments of need. When an opportunity arose to work as a Physician Assistant with a local doctor, I relocated to Casa Grande, Arizona, embarking on a new chapter of service.

It was there that I met Denice, the woman who would become my anchor. When she agreed to be my wife, I felt a happiness that rivaled even the joy of returning home from deployment. We eventually moved back to Iowa so I could further my education, and we were blessed with our daughters, Meredith and Maggie, who filled our home with laughter and purpose.

After returning to military service, I eventually retired in Arizona in 1996. Mother's passing in 1981 left a void in all our hearts. However, my father lived a remarkably long life in Ottumwa, nearly reaching his centennial before joining her. We have three grandsons, Colby, Bentley, and Grayson, who keep us young with their endless energy and curiosity. Denice and I celebrated our golden anniversary last September—fifty years that passed like a watch at sea, both endless and fleeting.

But perhaps the most profound moment of my later years came when I recently returned to my old ship, now a floating museum of steel and stories. Walking those decks again with Denice, our daughters, and my grandsons was like crossing between worlds. The boys ran from bow to stern, eyes wide with wonder, proudly announcing to everyone within earshot, "This is my Papa's ship!"

Standing on the aft elevator, I felt the years melt away. Tears welled in my eyes, not from sadness, but from the rush of memories so vivid I could taste the salt spray and hear the roar of aircraft. When I closed my eyes, I wasn't an old man anymore but that twenty-year-old sailor embarking on a journey most will never have or understand.

The ship and I are both showing our age now. But she remains as much a part of me as my heartbeat. Those years at sea shaped who I became—a husband, father, and grandfather.

The discipline and brotherhood I found in service carried me through life's storms, just as surely as the Midway carried me across distant waters.

As I watch another Arizona sunset fade into twilight, I'm grateful for the voyage—every port, every storm, every moment of calm seas that came into my life. The medals in my drawer mean less to me now than the memories etched in my heart and the legacy I see in my grandchildren's eyes when they look at me.

If any of my grandsons decide to join the service, I hope they join the Navy and have an adventure like their Papa's.